My Enemy, My Friend

Stories of
Palestinian and Israeli Christians
Working for Peace in
the Holy Land

Ellie Philpott

Sovereign World

Sovereign World Ltd
PO Box 777
Tonbridge
Kent TN11 0ZS
England

ISBN 1 85240 343 8

The publishers aim to produce books which will help to extend and
build up the Kingdom of God. We do not necessarily agree with every
view expressed by the author, or with every interpretation of Scripture
expressed. We expect each reader to make his/her judgement in the
light of their own understanding of God's Word and in an attitude of
Christian love and fellowship.

Cover design by CCD, www.ccdgroup.co.uk
Typeset by CRB Associates, Reepham, Norfolk
Printed by Clays Ltd, St Ives plc

Contents

Key to map

Dashed lines around the West Bank and Gaza are the 1949 Armistice Line.

Please note that the Palestinian territories outlined in this map are not entirely under Palestinian Authority control. Only 17% of the West Bank is under Palestinian Authority civil jurisdiction and security control. In 22% of the West Bank, the Palestinian Authority has civil jurisdiction, but Israel retains security control. The rest of the West Bank, approximately 60%, is under complete Israeli jurisdiction. Israel still retains ultimate authority over movement into and out of any area in the West Bank and can seal off any part of the West Bank at any time. Within the West Bank and Gaza Strip, Israel has also built over 240 illegal settlements and a number of by-pass roads. The United Nations has repeatedly affirmed that the Geneva Convention of 1948, which forbids the occupying power from transferring parts of its own civilian population into the territory it occupies, is applicable to the West Bank and Gaza Strip.

A certain man had two sons. One was rich and the other was poor. The rich son had no children of his own, whilst the poor son was blessed with many sons and daughters. One day the father fell ill. He was sure that he would not live through the week, so on Saturday he called his two sons to his bedside and gave them each half of the land of their inheritance. The old man died that day and before sundown the sons buried their father.

That night, the rich son couldn't sleep. He said to himself, "What my father did wasn't just. I am rich and my brother is poor. I have plenty of bread, while my brother's children eat one day and trust God for the next. I must move the boundary which our father has set in the middle of the land, so that my brother will have the greater share of our inheritance. Ah – but he mustn't see me doing this. If he sees me, then he will be shamed. I must get up early in the morning before dawn and move the boundary." With this, the rich son fell into a deep and peaceful slumber.

Meanwhile, the poor brother lay awake in his bed, saying to himself, "What my father did wasn't just. Here I am, surrounded by the joy of many sons and daughters while my brother daily faces the shame of having no sons to carry on his name and no daughters to comfort him in his old age. He should have our father's land. Perhaps this will in part compensate for his indescribable poverty. Ah – but if I give the land to him, he will be shamed. I must get up early in the morning before dawn and move the boundary which our father has set!" With this, the poor son fell into a deep and peaceful slumber.

On the first day of the week, very early in the morning, the two brothers met at the ancient boundary stones. They fell tearfully into each other's arms.

And on that spot was built the new Jerusalem.

> (Ancient saying quoted by a Jewish Rabbi)

Foreword

Today, Job gave me the idea for the foreword to this valuable little book. Job? What did he know about the conflict in the Middle East? Of course he did know about conflicts – big, life-threatening conflicts that affected him deeply, even though he didn't understand them.

Was it Jesse Penn-Lewis or Oswald Chambers who remarked that God and Satan had chosen Job's body and life as their battleground without letting Job know? Job's conflicts were way beyond the scope of his understanding – and even further beyond the understanding of his "friends", who didn't know God in the same way that Job did and so had only empty words to offer him.

To what extent are we observers, commentators or critics of the situation in the Middle East today? How far do we sympathize with one side or the other? No amount of knowledge qualifies us to be the ultimate umpire in this situation – no human could be impartial enough.

Today, in my daily reading, I saw Job's reply to his negative and critical friends, *"Have I not wept for those in trouble?"* (Job 30:25). Whatever standpoint we view – or have viewed – the situation from, I deny anybody the right to an opinion on the Middle East situation if they have not shed real tears for those in trouble. Whether or not we try to put the blame or credit on God (or Allah), the fact remains that wherever we turn in this conflict, we are confronted with the most terrible suffering. Every word of sympathy and support we try to offer just sounds hollow, superficial and sanctimonious.

Ellie and Sian have done a tremendous job in researching and describing the situation in the Middle East – I have seen for myself many similar incidents to those that are depicted here. That's why I would like to recommend this book to you. It doesn't offer the last word on this situation – but it does offer today's word. Without our compassion, no real understanding and help will come to the people on both sides who are caught up in this tragic conflict. We must ask ourselves the question, "Have I wept for them?" Maybe this little book will bring us to tears. That is my heartfelt prayer.

Brother Andrew
The Netherlands
September 2002

Introduction

I freely admit that in writing this book, I have tried to do the impossible! As Brother Andrew said in his foreword, nobody could ever be completely impartial when considering the Middle East problem. I am aware that supporters of both sides of this divide will find me easy prey for criticism. I have only given the bare bones of the historical and political situation in the Holy Land and in doing so, have not done true justice to the cause of either the Jews or the Palestinians.

However my intention is to give you food for thought and challenge your viewpoint, whatever it is, just as I have been completely challenged as I have traveled around the Holy Land and heard the stories of the people in this book. My intention is not to give a comprehensive analysis of the situation, but to provoke you to think – and hopefully to act.

My thanks must go to my family and friends who have supported and encouraged me throughout the process of writing this book. I am also grateful to Open Doors for so generously allowing me to use the research I carried out when working for them. I am indebted to the people in Israel and the West Bank who graciously shared their sorrows and joys with us, and who unfailingly showed us tremendous kindness and hospitality. But most of all, I am deeply grateful to my former colleague, Sian, for her patient explanations, her commitment to the people of the Holy

Land and for all her hard work in carrying out interviews, translation and research. Sian – this is your book just as much as it is mine.

Ellie Philpott
Oxford
August 2002

Chapter 1

Fraternizing with the Enemy

"O Jerusalem, Jerusalem, you who kill the prophets and stone those sent to you, how often I have longed to gather your children together, as a hen gathers her chicks under her wings, but you were not willing. Look, your house is left to you desolate. For I tell you, you will not see me again until you say, 'Blessed is he who comes in the name of the Lord.'"
(Matthew 23:37–39)

I looked up nervously as the security official nodded to me. It was my turn. Just around the corner from us, the Queen was standing in the garden, waiting to receive her guests – and I was one of them. I was really excited. Although I'm not the most ardent royalist around, it was quite something to meet the Queen in person. Just then, I glanced down and to my horror, realized I was wearing jeans. My hands felt clammy and my heart raced in panic – I couldn't meet the Queen of England in jeans! Where was the dress I had planned to wear? The official spoke again, and I looked up to see the Queen coming round the corner towards me. Suddenly, from a long way off, somebody began calling my name. It was my colleague, Sian, trying to wake me up. The whole thing was just a crazy dream.

For some obscure reason, I seem to have the most vivid dreams when I travel to the Middle East. Perhaps it is because I'm invariably woken by the Muslim call to prayer in the early hours of the morning. I sat up in bed musing over my latest dream – it wasn't difficult to work out where it had come from. The day before, just two days after our arrival in Amman, I had attended a Jordanian wedding in the city center. I hadn't anticipated going to an event of this kind when I'd packed my case for this trip and I'd been hard pushed to put together a halfway decent outfit for the occasion. I sat chuckling to myself, and then jumped up in horror. There was no time to waste – we were due to travel overland to Israel that morning and we needed to be at the Allenby Bridge border crossing in plenty of time to sort out our visas.

We stumbled bleary-eyed out of the guesthouse and hailed a taxi. By five thirty, we were engulfed in the chaos of Amman's central bus station. While Sian walked over to the central office to negotiate a rate for a *service* – one of the large shared taxis which are common all over the Middle East – I stood guard over our luggage, besieged by a horde of drivers, all fighting to grab our cases and tie them to their roof-racks. Fortunately Sian returned just before I was seriously in danger of losing the battle. We squashed ourselves into a battered old *service*, clambering over an interesting assortment of fellow passengers to get to the back seat, while our cases were being tied haphazardly onto the roof. As we pulled off, out of the graceful suburbs of Amman City, through the scrubland hills to the border, I prayed fervently that our luggage would make it safely with us to our destination.

Nearly two hours later we drew up at the Allenby Bridge border crossing – named after the British general who liberated Palestine from the Ottoman Turks in 1917. To my surprise, after all I'd heard about the zealous Israeli security checks, it was on the Jordanian side of the border crossing that we encountered problems. Our visas needed to be altered and the official was unhelpful. We were unceremoniously waved to the back of the queue and made to wait like naughty schoolchildren, while our fellow passengers tutted and squeezed past us. At last the official relented and with a quick glance at our faces, stamped our passports and pushed them towards us with an irritated sweep of his hand. Relieved, we made our way outside and scrambled onto the bus which took us over the Jordan river and a couple of hundred yards further to the Israeli side of the border. To my disappointment, the river was not much more than a small trickle at this point and I began to wonder if I was going to have to seriously revise my mental picture of the Holy Land.

A few minutes later, my first taste of Israeli security went like this:

"Where are you going?"

"Jerusalem, the West Bank – Bethlehem ..." I looked at the young soldier in what I hoped was wide-eyed innocence.

"What is the reason for your travel?"

"We've come to celebrate Christmas here." I confess now, I was somewhat economical with the truth. If I had told the soldier the true extent of our itinerary, which from an Israeli point of view would take in a suspiciously large number of forays into many flashpoints in the West Bank, we would have been standing at the border answering questions for a long time.

A smile transformed his previously guarded expression, "Merry Christmas. Welcome in Israel."

I grinned back, and walked on to retrieve my case. Sian was already outside in the sunshine. We stood in the shade waiting for a *service* to turn up, enjoying the pleasant cooling breeze. I glanced around us, catching sight of part of the border crossing reserved for vehicles. A large Toyota pickup was positioned over a service pit where two Israeli soldiers were examining the underneath, using mirrors on the end of long poles to check for bombs and weapons. Sniffer-dogs padded round the exterior of the car as the driver stood nearby, his hands in the air to allow the security officials to frisk him. It was a salutary reminder that we had just entered a conflict zone.

It didn't take long for a *service* to arrive and we eased our way inside. The driver crammed passengers in like sardines, until we all merged into a tangle of torsos, arms and legs. The *service* was stifling, my mouth felt dry and sweat began to trickle down my legs, but I couldn't reach my water bottle. Thankfully, the searing heat of the lush Jordan valley, filled with its avocado plantations and neat rows of date palms, soon disappeared behind us and the air grew cooler as the *service* climbed the Jericho road through the hills up towards Jerusalem, past scattered Bedouin tents and herds of long-eared sheep and goats. On the journey I struck up a conversation with the passenger sitting next to me, a slightly built, dark haired French woman in her forties. She was on her way back to Bir Zeit University in the West Bank from a visit to her boyfriend who lived in Jordan. To my fascination I discovered Céline was carrying out a research project on the position of women in Palestinian society. I bombarded her with questions for the next half an hour. "What I've found really fascinating," Céline told me, "are the changes that occurred during the *intifada* – the Palestinian uprising that happened in the late 1980s. During that time, young women fought alongside the men, doing very similar jobs to them. There was a real equality between them, which had rarely existed before in their society."

"What happened when the *intifada* ended?" I asked.

"That's the tragedy," was Céline's response. "The women just took up their old roles again. It was even harder for those who had been imprisoned during that time. Some of them had been raped in the prison camps by Israeli soldiers. When they returned to their villages, they were treated like outcasts. They couldn't be married because they'd become damaged goods. The same thing even happened to those who weren't raped because people believed the worst anyway. Many of the women I've spoken to are frustrated and bitter."

At last our taxi wound its way through the modern-day town that was once the little village of Bethany and before I knew it, we were rounding the Old City walls. Jerusalem was upon us.

I sat forward to get a better view of the city walls,

impressed by the elegance of the huge sand colored ramparts, which have survived relatively intact for centuries. To our right, just outside the walls, we passed the hill where the city of Jerusalem was located in King David's day. I wondered what had been going through his mind as he approached the city with his army, facing the Jebusites who jeered down from the city walls, taunting him. Undaunted by their jeers, David took advantage of a disused water shaft in the hill of Ophel, allowing Joab to climb up the duct into the city with a select band of armed men. Soon, his victorious army was in control and Jerusalem became the capital city of the united Israelite kingdom.

Our *service* creaked to a halt at the Damascus Gate. Sian glanced at me as we climbed out, stretching our cramped legs while we waited for our cases to be hauled off the roof.

"So, you've finally made it to the Holy Land. How do you feel Ellie?"

My work took me all over the world, and I was used to adjusting to new sights and sounds. I shrugged my shoulders. Israel didn't feel more important than any other country I had visited.

"Last year I brought a group of our directors here," she smiled, "One of them was in tears by the time we reached Jerusalem."

I felt vaguely guilty, as if I ought to have been more affected by our arrival in the city. But right then, I didn't have the energy to feel anything much but the rumblings of my hungry stomach and the desperate desire for a long, refreshing shower.

Sian waved at the huge gate behind us, eager to give me my first history lesson. "Did you know this gate was where the Crusaders finally broke into Jerusalem when they besieged the city?"

I racked my brains to try and think of what I could remember of the Crusades. Precious little, it turned out. Sian continued, "They slaughtered everybody inside – including the women and children. Apparently they even set fire to a synagogue where a group of Jews were hiding and watched them burn alive. After that, the Crusaders got down on their knees in the streets full of blood and bodies and kissed the ground that Jesus had walked on."

I grimaced; reminded of a cynical cartoon a friend had once copied for me. It showed a group of Crusader knights standing, swords at the ready, outside a Middle Eastern city. One of them was shouting up to the besieged Muslim occupants: "Hello, we've come to tell you about Jesus!" The sad thing is, part of the mistrust in the Arab world today towards Christians stems from the actions of the Crusaders. It is ironic that when the Islamic hero, Saladin, took Jerusalem from the Crusaders eighty years after their conquest, he showed far more mercy to its inhabitants than the Crusaders ever did.

I looked around me, enjoying the bustle of the Damascus Gate. In front of the huge stone portal, a large circular forum was filled with Arab traders selling sweets, nuts, spices, fruit and all kinds of vegetables, stacked on tables or laid out on cloths on the ground. At the top of the steps, boys were offering coffee and other drinks from brightly-colored handcarts. On the other side of the street from the gate, the buses for Bethlehem were pulled up at the curb-side in the shade of a broad avenue of palms. We walked back across the road to catch one to take us to our final destination – the Bible College in Bethlehem which was to be our base for the next couple of weeks. At the entrance to each bus, young Arab boys were rounding up passengers, good-naturedly vying for trade. It was a busy time of day. Women carrying huge baskets of fruit and vegetables were returning home from the market. The boys herded them into the waiting buses, calling out their destination as they did so: "Bet Lehem, Bet Lehem!" "Beit Jala!" "Gaza!" The strange names, shouted in heavily-accented Arabic, gave the whole scene an exotic flavor.

Sian hurried towards one of the buses that was nearly full and ready to leave. We heaved our heavy cases down the narrow aisle, and flopped onto the back seat, squashed between a sack of potatoes and some pineapples. Our fellow passengers glanced at us with friendly curiosity as we passed our shekels forward to the driver. It was quite unusual for Westerners to use local transport. I sat back, relieved to be on the last leg of our journey. Next and final stop, Bethlehem.

It was Christmas 1997 and I had come to Israel with a clear brief: to interview Christians, both Arab and Israeli, who were actively involved in reconciliation work. The second part of my task was to see whether the Christians on both sides were facing any kind of opposition to their faith from their own communities. I arrived in this part of the world with an embarrassingly small grasp of the history and politics of the region. Perhaps that was a good thing, as I think I had relatively few preconceived ideas as to what I would find. I was a blank sheet of paper, and very soon I was to find myself bombarded with stories, personal views and snippets of history from all points of view. It would take me a long time to begin to make sense of everything I'd heard.

What I did deliberately leave behind was any theological viewpoint I may have held. There are any number of books written by Christians on differing theologies concerning the Holy Land. I felt that in order to really get a grasp of the situation, I needed to hear from the Palestinian and Israeli Christians themselves, and to try and understand for myself the dynamics of life in this complex political situation. Only then would I return to theology.

I knew that the struggle between the Israelis and Palestinians reaches far back into history, and that in order to ever get a grasp of today's complex situation, I would need to understand some of the events that had taken place before. The fundamental issue is, of course, the claim by both Israelis and Palestinians to the land we now call Israel and the West Bank. Many – but not all – of the Israelis argue that this land was given to them by divine right when Jehovah led Moses and the entire Israelite nation from Egypt through the wilderness to the Promised Land. On the other hand, the Palestinians not only consider themselves descendants of the Arab conquerors who settled the land in the seventh century, but they also believe their descent goes back even further, to the people who were living in this land before the Israelite tribes arrived.

In fact, the situation is still more complex, as Alex Awad outlines in his little book, *Through the Eyes of the Victims*:

> "Let us take a look at the histories of many Muslims who now live in Palestine. The ancestors of some present day Muslims were Jewish at the time of Christ. Many of them became Christians after Christ proclaimed His Gospel and the Roman Empire adopted Christianity as the state religion. Finally, many of these Christians converted to Islam when Muslims conquered the Holy Land during the seventh century AD. In effect, many Arab Muslims in Palestine may have just as much if not more Jewish blood than the millions of Jews of European descent, who mixed and intermarried with Gentile Europeans for centuries."

So who has a right to the land? I wanted to find answers to my questions, but I didn't realize that my search through history would lead me to some very uncomfortable places indeed.

The first site I wanted to visit in Jerusalem was the Western Wall. So one afternoon, we came back from Bethlehem into Jerusalem. Later that day we had arranged to meet the first of our contacts, Cindy, who is a Messianic Jew – or Jewish believer in Jesus. We'd made our way to the Jaffa Gate in plenty of time to take a detour around the city. Above our heads, a flowing Arabic inscription was a potent reminder that Jerusalem has changed hands many times in the course of its long history. The words, "There is no God but Allah and Abraham is his friend," are thought to have been inscribed at the time the great walls were constructed in the sixteenth century by Turkish sultan Suleiman the Magnificent.

Much earlier on, after the death of King David, Jerusalem

passed into Solomon's hands, and the temple that he built was the awe of the known world. Tragically, a few generations later the Israelites had been sent into exile, and all that was left of the temple was a pile of ruins. Eventually they returned to the city, but they were never to know again the splendor of the days under the kingship of David and Solomon. The temple was later rebuilt by King Herod, and then destroyed again in AD 70 by the Romans when they ransacked the city following the Jewish revolt. Over the intervening years, the Jewish population living in Palestine dwindled until, by the sixteenth century, they numbered less than a thousand. It wasn't until the late 1880s that the Zionist movement began and Jews scattered throughout the world began to actively look for a homeland. The first Zionist colony in Palestine was founded in 1878 and the return of Jews to the Holy Land began in earnest.

In 1917, the British army rode into Jerusalem and it was at the Jaffa Gate that the commander, General Allenby, stopped, dismounted from his horse and walked into the Old City on foot to take control of Jerusalem, and eventually the whole of Palestine, from its Turkish rulers. This conquest set in motion a train of events that was to radically reshape the political structure of the entire country, and lead to a head-on collision between two nations fighting desperately for one territory.

As we stepped under the Jaffa Gate and into the old *souk*, I was entranced by the magical atmosphere of the Old City. We wandered into a warren of tiny stepped alleyways full of ancient boutiques selling all kinds of artifacts: mother-of-pearl crosses, leatherwork, brass ornaments, pottery, Hebron glass, religious icons and the checkered Arab headscarves known as *kaffiyehs*. The air was heady with the scent of spices. Here and there, wrinkled old men sat at tables tucked into the nook of an alleyway playing backgammon or draughts. As we climbed up the steps, young boys brushed past us, pushing handcarts with enormous loads. Suddenly we were brought up short. In the middle of the alleyway, next to a large metal detector and x-ray scanner, stood a group of Israeli soldiers, machine guns in their hands. I came back to the twentieth century with a jolt.

We emerged through the Israeli checkpoint into a vast expanse of plaza, momentarily dazzled by the intense light after the darkness of the *souk*'s alleyways. I looked up and saw in front of me the huge limestone blocks of the Western Wall rising way above my head into the sky. At the wall, Jews stood in prayer, heads pressed against the stones. Just in front of me, an elderly Hassidic Jew wearing a traditional long black coat and wide-brimmed hat had finished his prayers. He walked backwards away from the wall, his head bowed down until he reached the exit to the enclosure, then he stopped and raised his eyes up above the wall – there, gleaming in the sunlight, the golden Dome of the Rock blazed out its presence.

It brought home to me forcibly that Jerusalem is not only sacred to the Jews and the Christians but also to the Muslims who call this city *Al-Quds*, which means "the Holy". Above our heads stood Islam's oldest and third most important shrine, built in the eighth century by the city's Arab ruler, the caliph Abd al-Malik. Underneath the golden dome lies a slab of rock upon which, according to Islamic tradition, the Prophet Mohammed was lifted by Gabriel to paradise where he spoke with Adam, Jesus, the prophets and Allah before returning to spread the message of Islam to the world.

To the Jews this place is the holiest of holy places. The stones of the Western Wall are themselves part of the retaining wall of the Temple Mount, the only part of Herod's Temple complex to survive the Roman destruction. Above the wall, the Dome of the Rock is located on what once would have been the courtyards of Solomon's Temple itself. Only this section of wall has survived and has stood through the centuries, a focus for the longings of the Jews scattered throughout the world who desired one day to return to their homeland.

I was amazed to discover that these two holy sites lie

literally one on top of the other and began to see why Jerusalem in particular is such a hotly-contested city. I turned my back to the wall and scanned the broad sweep of plaza, noting the number of Israeli soldiers scattered around the area. Suddenly, the x-ray scanners made sense. Neither Palestinians nor Israelis could risk any kind of sabotage at this location – the result could well be all-out war.

We had time for a quick coffee before our appointment with Cindy, so we left the plaza and dived once more into the Old City. As we wandered along, trying to find our way through the mass of narrow alleys, Arab traders called out to us from their shops: "Come, come, you buy. Look, see – what you want? I give you good price." We stepped into one boutique, looking for pottery bowls. "My name is Mohammed. What's your name?" a smiling shopkeeper asked. "Ellie," I responded. That confused him. "Ali? Ali? That's a man's name!" We laughed with him.

We finally managed to track down the little café that Sian had been looking for. Inside, a young Palestinian was reading a copy of *Al Quds*, an Arabic daily newspaper. In the far corner, two elderly men sat crouched over a back-gammon board. One of them sucked idly at a water pipe. We opted for small cups of strong, sweet Arabic coffee flavored with cardamom pods and chatted to the café owner. Sian spoke very passable Arabic, as she had lived in the Middle East some years previously. The café owner was happy – there was relatively little trouble at the time and business was fairly good. Tomorrow, he reminded us, would be Ramadan, the Muslim month of fasting. "You come to the city at sunset and – bam!" he gestured an explosion, referring to the canon on the city walls which is fired at sunset to let the Muslims know their daily fast is over. "You come then, *inshallah* I will have good food."

We talked for a while longer, then paid the bill and left for our meeting. On the way, we walked through the Mahaneh Yehuda marketplace, where a Palestinian suicide bomber had recently blown himself up, killing and wound-ing a number of Israelis. It felt odd to be standing in the place that I'd seen on the news, at that time filled with ambulances, police and screaming people. Today, there was no sign of the attack, although I was all too aware that another suicide bomber could easily strike at any time anywhere in the city.

When we arrived at the Caspari Center where Cindy worked, we were greeted by a tall, lively woman with an unruly mop of graying curls. "Hi, I'm Cindy," she announced in a soft American accent. We had been given Cindy's name as a contact by Musalaha, a Christian reconciliation organization working in Israel and the West Bank. She had been involved in arranging their women's conference a few months previously. Articulate and amusing, Cindy was the perfect candidate to answer my questions.

I told her that we'd walked through the marketplace and asked how safe she felt, living and working in Jerusalem. Cindy grimaced, pointing from her window to the spot where the recent attack had occurred, saying, "You know, it's no wonder everybody is uptight here. I find that after the bombings happen, the next time you go out, you wonder if anything is going to happen. It really is scary on a human level." She sat down, leaning forward in her seat. "The whole cycle is self-perpetuating. After one of the bombings here downtown, I looked out of the window and heard some yelling from Jaffa Street, then I saw the soldiers. I think they wanted to check some Arab youth's ID. They were arguing, and they ended up dragging this kid down an alleyway. They didn't just hold his arm and walk him gently; they pushed him and were really rough with him and I thought, well, if you didn't hate Israelis before, you will now. But then you look at the soldiers and you think, okay a bomb went off a hundred meters from here yesterday, no wonder you're tense and suspicious . . . "

I asked Cindy what she thought were the long-term psychological effects on Israelis from Palestinian violence and suicide bombings:

"I know closing the borders to the West Bank won't stop somebody who really wants to get through with a bunch of explosives, but it helps us to feel more secure, a little bit more controlled. It is interesting, because the effects of the whole situation are much more obvious on the Palestinian side, and they are the ones who are suffering from it. They are basically oppressed. I think there is an effect on the Israelis, but it is more hidden, because our society is very Western, very modern. But there is a psychological trauma. The whole country is involved when something happens, the whole country mourns. And I imagine that almost everybody in this country has lost someone, either in a bombing or in a war or something. It is bad for both sides. And occupation itself is bad for the Israelis – it's not good for an eighteen-year-old Israeli boy to be stuck pointing a gun at an eighteen-year-old Palestinian boy."

I found myself wondering how I would react to the situation if I lived in Jerusalem. Would it make me more suspicious of people on the other side or would it push me towards them in an effort to do everything I could to facilitate peace? I couldn't say.

I asked Cindy how easy it was for her to meet with Palestinians.

"I think you have to step out to do it," was her response. "You have to make an effort, it doesn't happen naturally. There are the geographic boundaries too – for example it's not easy meeting Palestinian women from Bethlehem. Sometimes they can't get into Jerusalem because of border closures, and we can't get into Bethlehem either."

"The Musalaha women's conferences – what do you discuss there? The aim is to bring Messianic Jewish women and Palestinian Christian women together, isn't it?" I asked.

"Yes," Cindy replied, "at this last conference, we had a speaker who shared about her friendship with an Arab family who are not believers as an example of how we can reach out and be friends with people. And then the next day we had small groups, and the subject was general enough that people could talk about whatever they wanted – sharing our sorrows, sharing our joys. Some groups didn't touch on the political side of things at all, instead they shared the common things that women go through. My group happened to share a lot of hardships that are caused by the political situation. That was good. It is good to hear how people are going through things and how they are dealing with them, and to see how God is ministering to them and bringing joy out of it."

"So what would be the kind of reaction from other Jewish people living in Jerusalem when they hear about what you are doing?" was my next question. "Would you get opposition from them?"

"From the non believers?" Cindy was frank, "Yes, from some. They would say that we are fraternizing with the enemy and that our loyalties are divided. A lot would think it is a good thing. Unless people have a real vision to make peace, they don't have a lot of contact with the Arabs. That is a generalization, but it is uncomfortable: the tension on the two sides makes it like that. But as believers, our common ground takes us a step above where it is uncomfortable, so we can be together and even as we discuss these things, our bond is stronger than what divides us. I think if we can continue to meet together and if it can spread, then it will start to change things in society. That is what the Bible says after all – that the world will know that we belong to the Messiah and also will know that Jesus was sent by God, if we love one another – so I see it as our mandate. I think it could be the greatest witness among all, to see the peace that God can give."

Just then Cindy's phone rang and while she was talking, I picked up a leaflet on the table beside me which outlined the work of the Caspari Center. It made for interesting reading. The center was set up in the early 1980s to provide Biblical resources and study opportunities for Messianic Jews. In those days there were relatively few Messianic Jews living in Israel, and many of them had come to faith through Gentile Christians who gave them little teaching on how to work out their new faith within a Jewish context. Today, the center provides a much-needed resource for the expanding number of Messianic congregations in Israel, and also acts as a bridge between the Messianic community and the Christian community worldwide.

It was fascinating to think that the recent recreation of a Jewish State in the country of Israel has posed new problems of identity for the Jews themselves. Some are content to be living in Israel and don't feel the need to practice their faith in any other way. For them, the existence of a Jewish State is enough. Others, the religious Zionists, see the rebirth of the Jewish State as the first stage of a process that will culminate in the coming of the Messiah. For a number of these people, it isn't enough to occupy only part of the land. They believe the Messiah will only return after the Promised Land in its entirety is back in Jewish hands once more. Still others actively practice their faith, but see no need to possess the entire land and are happy to look for a solution that would enable them to live side by side with the Palestinians.

It is no wonder then that some of the Jewish converts to Christianity struggle to find an identity. It isn't necessarily straightforward to find a way of expressing their Christian faith within the context of their Jewish heritage – the struggles of the early Church bear witness to this fact. Cindy told us that she had emigrated from Israel in her twenties, and had become a Christian in the United States, where she met her husband Sean. They had only returned to Jerusalem a few years previously. When she finished her phone call, I asked Cindy how she felt about her own conversion to Christianity:

"There has been a lot of bad blood between the Jews and the Church for many years," she responded. "It is a difficult issue for a lot of people. I feel very blessed that I met the Lord in a way that was outside the considerations of being Jewish. I went to a very balanced church in the States with good fundamental teaching. I am thankful for that because many people here have a lot of questions about their identity in the Messiah."

I wanted to know whether Cindy thought the Messianic

Jews in Israel felt isolated and threatened by other sections of the Jewish population.

"Well, we're a kind of non-entity," was her response. "Most people don't know that we exist. If they know we exist, they don't know a whole lot about us, although that is changing slowly. I had a funny encounter with my landlady more than three years ago when we first moved into our apartment here. After a month, I mentioned something to her about our congregation and she started asking me what congregation. 'Oh!' she said, 'You're believers, I didn't know. I wouldn't have guessed!' It was kind of funny – she may have expected me to wear a nun's habit or something or a tattoo on my forehead. It was just a very strange reaction: 'Well you *seem* like a normal person ...'" Cindy paused for a moment, then continued: "We have some Orthodox neighbors who became less friendly when they found out we were Messianic Jews ... but in general, other than the Orthodox people, who really have a kind of personal aversion to Christianity for what-ever reason, most people really don't mind. 'You can believe whatever you want, just don't push it on me' seems to be the general attitude."

The time we spent with Cindy went quickly and I realized I'd grown to like her sense of humor and engaging honesty. Reluctantly we left her office and, with still a little time to spare, walked to our final destination before home, the Via Dolorosa. Although this alleyway section of the Old City is not the real path that Jesus took on His way to the cross, it serves as a potent symbol for tourists, and at any time of the day you are likely to see groups of pilgrims – some carrying crosses, others crying or on their knees, and some standing quietly in contemplation.

Sadly, experiencing the Holy Land sites at first hand can prove too much for some pilgrims. Jerusalem Syndrome is a diagnosed medical condition in which a small minority of visitors to the city become so caught up in the experience that they begin to believe they are the reincarnation of some religious figure. The authorities have had to develop a tactic for dealing with these unfortunates – they are taken to a hospital outside the city and eventually shipped home. At any one time, the hospital may well contain a couple of John the Baptists, a Mary Magdalene and even a Jesus himself.

Earlier, we had asked Cindy how she thought the Jewish residents of the city viewed its pilgrims. "They think they're nuts!" was her reply. "I'll tell you a joke. It's actually a true story, which my husband heard from a friend of ours who is a tour guide. He was with a group of tourists and was telling them about the particular location where they were. He asked if they had any questions and one woman spoke up and said, 'This is all very interesting, but can you tell me why there are so many Jewish-looking people around?'"

Chapter 2

Survivors

"In Germany they came first for the Communists, and I didn't speak out because I wasn't a Communist. Then they came for the Jews and I didn't speak out because I wasn't a Jew. Then they came for the trade unionists and I didn't speak out because I wasn't a trade unionist. Then they came for the Catholics and I didn't speak out because I was a Protestant. Then they came for me, and there was no-one left to speak for me."

(German pastor, Martin Niemöller,
who spent eight years imprisoned in
Nazi concentration camps.)

"Ahlan wasahlan – welcome, welcome. Please come in. Do you like Arabic coffee? I'll get you some." The smiling gray-haired man greeted us with typical Middle Eastern hospitality. Sian grinned and shook his hand warmly. "Bishara, it's good to see you again," she said, and I realized who the slightly-built Palestinian standing in front of us was: Bishara Awad, President of the Bethlehem Bible College. I tried to guess how old he was, perhaps in his late fifties I thought, but he had that kind of ageless face that made it hard to discern.

We sat down and Selwa, Bishara's wife, appeared with tiny cups of black Arabic coffee and a bowl of dates. "So, you had a good journey?" Bishara enquired.

"No trouble," replied Sian. "The borders are quiet at the moment."

"Yes, it is a good time to be here. Let's hope it will last," was Bishara's response.

I thought back to the last stage of our journey, crossing the border into the West Bank. Our bus had pulled out of the busy city center traffic at the Damascus Gate in Jerusalem and onto the main road towards Bethlehem. As we drove around the city wall and down a steep hill, I caught sight of a man on a white Arab horse galloping along the valley below us. I blinked my eyes, and he had already disappeared, following the path underneath a little bridge spanning the valley. I came to realize this curious juxtaposition of old and new is a strange feature of the Holy Land. Just when I was struggling to reconcile the modern day urban landscape with the Bible scenes I had grown up with, I would come across a scenario that could have happened two thousand years ago. A man broadcasting seed in a field tilled by yoked oxen, women in long traditional embroidered dresses and headscarves, carrying vegetables home from the market, or a wizened old shepherd walking in front of a flock of long-eared sheep and goats.

On the short journey to Bethlehem, I tried to work out where we were in relation to the Palestinian territories. Today they consist of the Gaza Strip – a narrow swathe of land on the Mediterranean coast – and the West Bank – 5,860 square kilometers of land stretching along the Jordan River to the east, northwards into the valleys of Samaria and south into the Judean Hills. We were headed south into the Judean countryside. On our left I spotted an old monastery situated on top of a hill. By the side of the road, a signpost pointed towards Bethlehem using the indigenous spelling of the town's name, Bet Lehem, which means "House of Bread". Just then we dipped down into a small valley and up the other side, easing to a halt at the checkpoint which marked the end of Israel and the beginning of the West Bank. Red and white plastic barrels across the road prevented our bus from driving straight through.

A few young Israeli soldiers stood by the barrels, their guns slung over their shoulders. As they glanced at the occupants of our bus, I caught sight of a beautiful garden set on the hillside next to the road, enclosed by a long stone wall. All of a sudden, I spotted three or four teenage Palestinian boys running along the other side of the wall. I nudged Sian, who quietly explained, "There's very little work in the West Bank, so a large number of the Palestinians have to find jobs in Israel in order to survive. The problem is, many of the older teenagers can't get permission from the Israeli authorities to leave the West Bank, as they're just the right age to be militants or suicide bombers. So they sneak out the back way ... "

Our bus lurched forwards and eased its way around the barrels. On the other side of the checkpoint, the road was crammed with parked cars all with a distinctive blue number plate, indicating that the cars were registered in the West Bank and that the owners couldn't take them into Israeli territory. Instead, the Palestinians had to drive to the border, cross on foot and travel by public transport the other side. It seemed a funny sort of world to me, where the color of your number plate defined where you could or couldn't drive.

On the Hebron Road – the main access route into the center of Bethlehem – I spotted a bus pulled up at the curbside next to a long high wall. A group of Orthodox Jewish women were climbing out and walking through a narrow door set into the wall, which was guarded by a couple of Israeli soldiers. Jewish women in the West Bank? I was even more confused. It was unusual for Jews to be found quite so conspicuously in Palestinian territory. Once again, Sian took on the role of tour guide, and explained that they were visiting Rachel's Tomb, a monument built on the site where Jacob's wife is said to be buried. In 1841, a British philanthropist, Sir Moses Montefiore rebuilt the dome over the tomb. Now, judging by the building work taking place around the dome, the Israelis were extending his edifice. Sandbags were piled up on the flat roofs of the buildings on either side of the road and above our heads an Israeli soldier stepped into view, watching over the tomb. "Or, from the Palestinian perspective, taking advantage of a handy foothold in the West Bank," remarked Sian. "It all depends from which side of the fence you view things."

I discovered later that this particular spot just outside Rachel's Tomb is one of the major flashpoints in Bethlehem. Here the road forks, with the Hebron Road continuing to the right and Manger Street on the left-hand side leading to Manger Square where the Church of the Nativity is located. When trouble flares up in the West Bank, Palestinian boys build barricades across one or both of the roads, sheltering behind them to throw stones at the soldiers guarding Rachel's Tomb. The Kand Company petrol station on our left bore witness to this – a good half of the tiles were missing from the roof, and stray bullets had punched holes into the metal infrastructure underneath the canopy. It became a joke for us – on subsequent trips to the West Bank we would look to see how many more tiles were missing from the roof, until the day came when we were caught up in the fighting here ourselves. Suddenly it wasn't funny any more.

Our bus took the right-hand fork along the Hebron Road and soon Bethlehem Bible College appeared on our right, directly opposite the al Azza refugee camp. We shouted to the driver and the bus pulled to a halt just outside the main entrance.

The afternoon was sunny, and with nothing scheduled for the rest of the day, we decided to walk into the town center to have a look around and visit the Church of the Nativity. In common with a lot of visitors to the Holy Land, I was completely surprised by the town of Bethlehem. Naively, I had expected to find myself in the middle of the tiny village which slumbers on the front of our Christmas cards. Modern-day Bethlehem was very different indeed. Cars, banks, cafés – I was greeted by all the hustle and bustle of a twentieth century Arab town.

We decided to take the back route to Manger Square and

turned off the noisy street punctuated every ten minutes or so by huge air-conditioned tourist buses, which stopped off at the large gift shops en route before heading for the Nativity Church. I looked curiously as the occupants of the buses were herded into the smart air-conditioned stores. Just as we walked past one, a group of Japanese tourists were milling through the shop. We followed them in to have a look, but I felt curiously detached, aware that I wasn't here as a tourist. It was a feeling that would follow me insistently whenever I returned to this part of the world on my research trips. I felt as if I occupied some kind of shadowy existence, wandering in and out of people's lives. They spoke to me about their situation, but I gave relatively little information back about myself in return. I didn't feel part of any community. It was a weird sensation, as if I was just there to absorb feelings, stories and events that happened around us – a kind of human sponge. At one point I reached overload and had to be debriefed, before I was completely overwhelmed by the sadness of everything that I'd seen. But that was in the future.

Now, we were wandering up a winding road into the older parts of Bethlehem. On either side of the street, balconies overhung the pavement. We passed a wrinkled old woman shelling peas into a basket on one balcony. On another, teenage girls sat and talked, keeping a watchful eye on events in the street below. Soon we found ourselves walking steeply upwards as the road grew narrower and narrower, turning into a small alleyway that brought us out into the meat market. The market had long finished, but pools of blood lay in the narrow concrete channels, waiting to be sluiced down. The sickly sweet smell and swarms of buzzing flies were overwhelming and we quickly turned down another alleyway. Just further on we stopped to buy *falafel* at a stall and sat to eat them at the edge of a little cobbled road. Arabs passing by gave us curious glances – it would have been completely out of culture to find two Arab women doing likewise. I was aware of the strangeness of everything around me. I knew very few of the rules that governed Arab society and I began to grow nervous of giving offence.

It brought it home forcibly just how different the Arab and Israeli cultures are. To the Arabs, the Western – sometimes almost brash – Israeli lifestyle, lived at an often frenetic pace seems overwhelming and utterly foreign. The Israelis find it equally difficult to understand the complexities of the more tribal Arab culture.

The twisting alleyway finally brought us out into Manger Square – a huge white stone plaza, shining in the afternoon sun. In front of us lay the vast, sprawling Church of the Nativity, supposedly located over the cave where Jesus was born; on our right, streams of people buzzed in and out of an arcade of tourist shops. To our backs was the Mosque of Omar, its huge minaret soaring upwards to the sun. I was shocked to see a mosque in this of all places until I remembered that nowadays the population of Bethlehem is largely Muslim.

The square was quiet that afternoon, but a week later on Christmas Eve it was heaving with people. Sitting in the middle in a cordoned off area was a gathering of tourists and dignitaries, there to watch the choirs who perform annually outside the Church of the Nativity. Elsewhere in the square, young people – predominantly Palestinian teenage boys – milled around, laughing and having fun. At one point, a little boy stumbled at my feet, and two enormous brown liquid eyes peered up at me from behind a curly white false beard. He was wearing a Father Christmas outfit – many sizes too big for him – tied around the waist with a piece of string. In his hand he held tightly onto a little bell. The boy picked himself up and ran off in the direction of yet more mini Father Christmases, jingling the bell as he did so. Although many of these young people are Muslim and don't celebrate Christmas as a religious festival, Christmas Eve is a carnival for them – a rare chance to have some fun.

The previous evening, we had helped friends at the Bible College prepare the packages which were now being handed out to the crowds. Each contained a copy of a gospel, a tract and a response form. Some of the packages already lay discarded on the ground – the man in the *falafel* store later complained to us about the mess. But I did see other packages tucked surreptitiously into a pocket or a bag. Just one month later, over six hundred response forms had been returned, all requesting more information about Jesus.

On this peaceful sunny afternoon, we walked into the Church of the Nativity, bending down to pass under the low doorway of the Gate of Humility. I struggled to see any religious significance in the ornate church structures that confronted our eyes, all too aware of the petty in-fighting that still takes place between the three different Christian denominations which run the site. In the crypt underneath the Greek Orthodox side of the church lies the spot where Jesus is said to have been born. If you enter through the Roman Catholic side of the church, and descend into the subterranean chapels, you will eventually come across an anonymous wooden door, built to prevent the Roman Catholics from gaining access to the holy place. I'm afraid to say I once carved my initials on the door, in a passionate fit of anger at the petty divisions in the churches, which obscure the true message of the gospel.

When we returned to the Bible College we spent some time talking with Bishara. I quickly warmed to this gentle, earnest man. His passion to show God's love and mercy to his fellow Palestinians was clear to see. It was Bishara who founded the Bible College to encourage Palestinian Christians to stay and witness in the West Bank, rather than leave for a better life abroad. A few years ago he started up the Shepherd Society, an organization devoted to relief work amongst the Christian and Muslim communities in the Bethlehem area.

I asked Bishara to tell us something of his own story and he began with the tragic events of 1948. It was the end of the British Mandate in Palestine. British rule had begun thirty years earlier, when General Allenby's army, aided by the Arabs, captured Palestine from the Ottoman Turks in

1917. In return for their help, the British promised independence to the Palestinians. At the same time the British made another strategic alliance to bolster their position in the First World War – they guaranteed the Zionist Jews a Jewish homeland in Palestine.

Britain's contradictory promises became increasingly difficult to sustain and throughout the next thirty years they favored first one side then the other. The Palestinians grew more and more nervous as the number of Jewish immigrants swelled beyond all estimates and the British government's initial pro-Zionist stance became evident. By mid 1936 the Palestinians had embarked upon a full-scale violent rebellion. The British army, aided by Zionist militia groups, brutally crushed the rebellion. Ironically, it was the British who began to train the Zionists for combat and amongst the militia were many of Israel's future leaders.

Political events on the world stage took a turn for the worse. The threat of increasing hostilities from Nazi Germany once again pushed Britain to seek allies in the Middle East. In a concession to the Palestinians (the British badly needed Arab oil and fighting support), they decided to limit the number of Jewish immigrants into Palestine and promised that a Palestinian state would be established within ten years. This move alienated the Zionists – all the more so as Britain and America were themselves refusing to take in the vast numbers of refugee Jews from Germany and Europe who were fleeing the atrocities there. Now it was the turn of the Zionists to rebel against the British administration. A number of terrorist attacks against British troops led to an ever more unstable situation, augmented by increasing unrest between the Jews and Palestinians. In 1947 the British threw the "problem" of Palestine over to the United Nations. The final solution was to partition the land into two – a Jewish state which would occupy fifty two percent of the land and a Palestinian state which would encompass the remaining forty eight percent. Jerusalem and its environs would become an international zone.

The Jews, whose portion contained much of the best farming country, were ecstatic. The Palestinians, by far the majority population, were devastated and refused to accept the partition plan. By the time Britain pulled out of Palestine in 1948, the hostilities between the two nations were developing into full-scale war. The Jews, whose troops were much better organized and equipped, quickly gained the upper hand over the Arabs.

"I remember 1948 clearly," Bishara told us. "It was the year my father died. I was only nine, and all around us the troops on both sides were fighting for territory. We were sheltering in our house in Musrara, just a little walk away from the Damascus Gate, when my father stepped out of the house and was shot dead. We are not even sure if he was killed by Jews or Arabs. There was nothing we could do for him. We couldn't even take his body to the cemetery as it was too dangerous to leave the house. Instead, we had to bury him in the courtyard behind our house. There was no priest so my mother, who was a Christian, read from the Bible and said a prayer. Then we all joined in the Lord's Prayer.

"We were under siege for many weeks together with twenty other families. Eventually we began to run out of food and my mother remembered there was some foodstuff on the third floor of the house, but we couldn't get there from the inside. She was courageous – she was the only one prepared to climb to the third floor from the outside stairs. The soldiers shot at her and broke the steps underneath her. She made it inside the third floor and the soldiers continued to shoot through the windows. She told us later that she built a fire in the room to make them think the house had caught fire and she'd died as a result, but in actual fact she passed the food to us from the back of the house. After that we were moved by the Jordanian army to the Old City and that was the last time we saw our home."

Needless to say, Bishara was profoundly affected by these events. When he was older, he emigrated to the United States to pursue theological studies. He then returned to the

West Bank and married Selwa, a Palestinian Christian from Gaza. In 1972, they came to the little town of Beit Jala on the outskirts of Bethlehem to run a school for deprived Palestinian boys.

"It was a place of pain," Bishara recalled. "The boys, all of them Palestinians, had each suffered in one way or another from the harsh treatment associated with the Israeli occupation. Hatred welled up in me and I felt powerless to help the students come to terms with their own struggles, because of the anger and bitterness in my own life.

"One night, I cried out to God, tears pouring down my face. I asked for forgiveness for hating the Jews and for allowing that hatred to control my life. That evening, I felt God's presence in a new way. In an instant, He took away the hatred, the frustration and hopelessness and transformed it into love."

Bishara is one of many Palestinian Christians who face the daily challenge of practicing their faith under enormously difficult circumstances. He would be the first to say that forgiveness towards those who hurt you is an ongoing process. Equally, Bishara isn't afraid of speaking out on behalf of his people: "We feel that as Palestinian Christians, we need to stand for peace, justice and human rights and if we see injustices we need to speak against them – whoever is perpetrating them. We certainly need to be peacemakers and live as Jesus told us in the Beatitudes, but if the Palestinians are needy we will give to them. If someone is in jail and we visit him – as Jesus said we should – that can be explained as a political statement. So many times we do not intend to be in politics, but we find ourselves in a situation where evil is really creeping into the land and we feel we should speak against evil."

I wanted to know what Bishara's message was to other Christians around the world. "Please," he said, "please pray for the Palestinian Christians. Sometimes it hurts us so much when we see Christian pilgrims coming to the Holy Land and they visit all the sites – the monuments and churches – but they ignore the living Church. Some of them are even unaware that Palestinian Christians exist. Many, many Arab Christians are emigrating from the West Bank and Gaza because life is so tough here and now we are only a tiny minority – we desperately need your support and prayers. Otherwise who will witness to our Muslim neighbors here? But please understand me – I am not saying don't pray for the Jews. On the contrary, we pray for the Jews and we love them. All I ask is that you remember the Palestinian Christians here as well."

Another of the many people caught up in the events of 1948 was a young Jewish soldier called Josef Ben Eliezer. Almost fifty years afterwards, in December 1997, Josef came to the West Bank on an extraordinary act of reconciliation. Whilst I was there, I had the privilege to meet him at the Bible College and hear his story first hand.

On 13th July 1948, Josef was a member of the Israeli army unit that ransacked the village of Lod – the Lydda of the Bible. Josef had returned now, some fifty years later, with the intention of visiting a Palestinian Christian in the town who was there during the fighting in 1948. He wanted to ask forgiveness for the acts of cruelty carried out by the Israeli troops. Josef's story began in Europe in the years leading up to the Second World War:

"I was born in Frankfurt in 1929," he told us, sitting cross-legged in a low chair, his gaze fixed in the past. "My parents were Eastern European Jews who had emigrated to Germany from Poland to escape the persecution and poverty there. When I was only three years old, I remember looking out of our window down onto the Ostendstrasse. As I gazed onto the street, a group of young men in uniform marched past our house, singing. The words drifted up to us on the breeze – I can still see the horror on my parents' faces as they realized what the men were singing: 'Wenn Judenblut vom Messer spritzt,' – when Jewish blood runs from our knives . . . "

Josef's family returned to Poland but even there they couldn't escape the German troops. In 1939 they were rounded up and marched off by the soldiers, who searched them brutally and took away their money and valuables. Eventually Josef's family made it safely to Siberia, where his mother died of typhoid.

"At the age of fourteen, I found myself completely alone in the world," he said. "I escaped to Palestine, hoping to make a new life for myself. The year was 1943. I was filled with anger and bitterness, which was only fuelled by the behavior of the British Administration. How dare they restrict the immigration of Holocaust survivors! How could they show so little sympathy to us! But when they left in 1948 the fighting began in earnest. I was nineteen and desperate for action. We Jews were determined never, never to let these things happen to us again. I joined an elite corps of the army and one day my unit was stationed at a village called Lod. The villagers had been ordered to leave by the Israeli army, but to my colleagues' minds they weren't leaving fast enough. My detachment was based at the edge of Lod on a dirt road which was the main exit point. When the Palestinians came to our control post, they were checked. Their money was taken and some of my colleagues used very brutal methods. I could see what was happening to the people – when I was ten years old the same thing happened to me and I knew exactly what they were going through. What especially struck me were the people with small children. I couldn't understand that we were doing the same thing to them that was done to us. They were also children of God!"

Josef paused and put his head in his hands, overwhelmed by the emotions his memories evoked. After a while he continued, "I was shocked by what happened in Israel. I didn't want to be a part of that, so I left the country. I met a group of people who showed me Christian love in Jesus and I saw how they experienced their faith in a good way. Suddenly I understood Jesus and how He wanted to bring people together. He wants to reconcile people and He calls the whole world to come to Him and to unite and to live in harmony. I dedicated my life to that and that's why I have come to Israel. Because of the enormous power that Jesus has to bring people together as a testimony that there is a different way."

For Josef, the meeting with the Palestinian Christian had been an emotional time, and I hope and believe that God used the encounter to heal them both from the pain of their memories. For me, our chance encounter with Josef was enough to show me that there are so many different sides to this conflict and I began to realize how dangerous it was to align myself with one side or the other. Already I was overwhelmed with the suffering I saw in the lives of the Palestinians, but my encounter with Josef helped me to understand a little of the history of the Jews too and to grasp something of the enormity of the suffering they have gone through.

I encountered a number of other people during those first two weeks that I spent in Israel and the West Bank, all with similar stories to those of Josef and Bishara, stories of pain and hardship. At times the sadness engulfed me, and it was then that Bethlehem took on a new guise for me. As I wandered around the streets in my spare time, I thought of Jesus and the situation into which He was born. I realized that He too knew the pain and frustration of occupation – just like Josef and Bishara. Jesus faced the challenge of living out His faith in a world of political intrigue, injustice and uncertainty. And His solution of love and forgiveness reaches through two thousand years to the present day.

Chapter 3

Growing up in Gaza

"We don't have a single child in Gaza who knows what it is like to be a normal child."

(Abdul Rahman Bakr,
Director of Gaza City's psychiatric hospital,
Time magazine, 27 May 2002.)

We edged into the cramped office to collect our passports. They were lying in a heap in front of us on the bare wooden desk. The Israeli soldier picked them up one by one and flicked through the pages in silence. Then he pushed the passports towards us and asked with genuine curiosity, gesturing at the desolate expanse of bare concrete outside his window, "Why do you want to go to Gaza? There is nothing there, you know."

I almost believed him. The Eretz border crossing where we were standing was one of the bleakest places I had ever traveled through. On either side of the crossing point, huge white concrete walls topped with spirals of barbed wire rose high into the sky. In between, a wide tarmac road stretched its way past a jumble of security sheds and tiny offices towards what is, in effect, a vast, 360 square kilometer prison camp.

We collected our passports in relief – I have known friends to be stuck at this particular checkpoint for a very long time. The hour we'd had to wait was nothing. Outside, the blazing sunshine bounced off the concrete and tarmac with a dizzying brightness, blinding us for a few seconds. It took us five minutes or so to walk along the stretch of no-man's land until we reached the Palestinian checkpoint. The only other sign of life was a solitary lorry, its contents spewed out on the pavement as Israeli guards swarmed over the empty trailer searching for bombs or illegal weapons.

The Palestinian border guards glanced at our passports, wrote our names down in a little notebook and waved us on silently, their faces grave. I was surprised, used to the friendly greetings and smiles from the West Bank border guards who are usually pleased to see Western tourists entering their territory. But here in the middle of so much nothingness, there seemed little to smile about.

At the other side of the checkpoint, a few battered taxis were pulled up next to a bus shelter. In the shade, the drivers stood smoking and talking desultorily to one another. A stout elderly man in an old suit jacket and *kaffiyeh* (head-scarf) peeled away from his friends and hailed us. We negotiated a fare for Gaza City, a short distance from the Eretz checkpoint.

"Welcome in Gaza. This is your first time here? Welcome. You are tourists? On business?"

"Some business, some tourism," we replied and he raised an eyebrow, glancing at us in the driving mirror.

I slammed the passenger door shut and we pulled away from the border at an alarming speed, racing along a road that led through sand dunes and a mass of construction, swerving to avoid little donkey carts and dumpster trucks. Gaza is one of the most overcrowded spots on this earth, with over a million people crammed into a space slightly more than twice the size of Washington D.C. Every year, more precious agricultural land is sacrificed to provide housing for an ever-increasing population, many of whom lack the necessary permits to emigrate from the Gaza Strip – and a good number would be only too glad to leave.

On the short ride into Gaza City we passed the Jabalya refugee camp, one of eight camps in the Strip that house vast numbers of displaced Palestinians. In 1948, over two hundred thousand Palestinian refugees poured into Gaza, seeking shelter from the fighting. At the time, many of them thought their stay would last two or three weeks at the most. Today, the majority are still here, huge extended families crowded into tiny breeze block rooms, often with little sanitation and very poor quality water supplies.

As we passed the Jabalya camp, we saw young children in scruffy clothes running around barefoot in the dirt and sand. Women were squatting down cooking the family meal over small kerosene stoves, shooing the endless swarms of flies away from their cooking pots. An assortment of donkeys, sheep, chickens and goats wandered through the narrow alleyways, picking through the piles of rubbish that lay uncollected at the end of the street. The women looked at us as we passed, returning our curious stares with their own. I glanced away, embarrassed to be a spectator of their poverty. I had intended to take photographs of the refugee camps to remind myself later of what they looked like, but I couldn't bring myself to take away any more of these people's dignity.

As we passed from the sprawl of crumbling buildings and piles of rubble into the broader streets of central Gaza City, I thought I could catch a faint echo of the thriving port that once existed in this spot. It is ironic that Gaza's unique location, here at the gateway to many ancient civilizations, has proved to be the making – and breaking – of the city, time and again.

Throughout the centuries, people from a vast array of cultures and civilizations have passed through Gaza, some for the simple purpose of trade, others with a view to using the city's strategic position as a primary outpost for conquest of the rich, fertile land to the east. Egypt in particular has played a major role in Gaza's history, as successive pharaohs have conquered the city, demanding tributes of oils, spices and camels from its beleaguered occupants. In 35 BC, Gaza was even given as a gift from Mark Anthony to Cleopatra.

We stopped the taxi in the center of town and wandered

around the streets to get a feel of the place, heading towards
the coast. As we turned down a side street, we bumped into
a group of young schoolgirls on their way home for the
afternoon. They were dressed in jeans and identical green
smock tops with a little white ruff, each girl with a rucksack
on her back and a cheeky grin on her face. They crowded
round us with the boldness and curiosity of young children, eager to speak with us. I guessed they didn't see many
visitors to the Gaza Strip.

"What is your name? Hello, hello!" they cried out in
broken English. We stopped and chatted to them for a
while. It reminded me of a similar occasion in Bethlehem
when I had bumped into a group of schoolgirls in the
Hebron Road. The Bethlehem girls were much older and
our conversation had taken a rather more political turn. I
had innocently asked the eldest girl what she wanted to do
when she left school. "I want to be a human rights lawyer."
"Why?" I asked. "So I can defend my people and fight for
the oppressed," came the reply.

The road down to the seashore was covered with a thin
layer of sand, which had drifted inland from the beach.
Every now and then donkeys clopped past us pulling small
makeshift carts loaded with sheep, vegetables, tires and all
manner of goods. The streets on either side of us were
dismal – plaster was peeling from the crumbling buildings
and on the wall beside us somebody had spray-painted
Hamas logos and other militant slogans. Just around the
corner, we were stopped in our tracks by the haunting
image of a young black-haired Palestinian boy painted onto
the wall. He was dressed in a khaki jacket and next to his
face was written his name: Hamdi Abu Hasira, together
with the date that he met his death as a *shahid* or martyr to
the Palestinian cause: 17th January 1993. Hamdi's dark eyes
stared blankly at us, and a patch of crumbling plaster
underneath one eye looked like a single teardrop falling
down his cheek. We walked past the wall and on towards
the beach.

Even the sight of the sea wasn't particularly cheerful. The

sandy beach in front of us was piled high with rubbish and the rubble from a half-demolished building. A solitary breeze-block wall remained standing with a gap where the doorframe had once fitted. Through the empty doorway, I could see the rusting burnt-out wreck of a car half covered by the drifting sand. I glanced out to sea, catching sight of a group of little boats in the distance, bobbing on the waves just as the sun broke through a layer of brooding cloud, its rays sending jets of light sparkling over the water.

I wondered what life must be like for those young schoolgirls growing up in Gaza, with so little hope for any kind of a future. Selwa, Bishara Awad's wife was born in Gaza City, and one afternoon a few years later, when we were sheltering in the Bible College, trapped by fighting outside, we persuaded Selwa to tell us her story. Her eyes twinkled in animation as she spoke, her rich voice drawing out the vowels in the Arabic way. Selwa's story bubbled out of her as she remembered the past:

"In 1948 I was three years old. My father decided to leave Gaza and to go to Egypt because the fighting between the Israelis and Palestinians was too much. We lived in Port Said for a year while my father looked for a job – he was a dentist. But he didn't find any work, so eventually we returned to Gaza."

When Selwa and her family came back to the city in the early 1950s it was to a new occupying force. As a result of the Arab-Israeli hostilities in 1948, Israel now occupied 77% of Palestine. Jordan had taken control of the West Bank of the Jordan River and of East Jerusalem. The Gaza Strip had come under the authority of Egypt.

"During that time, the United Nations came to Gaza to help the refugees," Selwa told us. "My father applied for work as a dentist with the UNWRA – the United Nations Works and Relief Agency – that had been specially set up to help the Palestinians in Gaza. They hired him and we lived in Gaza Town. Gaza is a very strict Muslim community, so as Christians we had to be respectful of their customs. For example, we were careful how we dressed, not wanting to offend our neighbors. Once my friend was wearing a gold cross around her neck when we were out walking and somebody came up to her and tore it off her. I never wore a cross outside my clothes after that. But my family had many friends among the Muslims and we got on okay with them. My father was well known in Gaza – he was nice with everybody. If you go to him for treatment and you don't have any money, you would tell him and he would say okay, no problem. This is how he showed Christian love to the people, and they respected us."

Most Gazans were reasonably content with the Egyptian administration. For one thing, they were fellow-Arabs and were far more sympathetic to the Palestinian culture than the British had been. Indeed, it was quite common for Egyptians and Gazans to intermarry. "The Egyptians used to come to Gaza and rent places there," Selwa told us. "Because there was no tax, it was very attractive for them. They would come and buy our products, which were very cheap for them and good quality. It was okay during the Egyptian time. I know a lot about Egypt because when we were growing up in Gaza, everything was Egyptian." An added bonus to the Gazans was that they were allowed to study in Egyptian universities. A wealth of new opportunities was opening up to them.

Selwa was one of the Palestinians who benefited from the Egyptian administration. Taking advantage of the improved educational facilities, which had been rudimentary under the British Mandate, she studied to become a teacher. "I was teaching the first grade for three years – and we used to work hard! It's not like you – we had maybe forty, forty-five students in each class. When they came to me, they didn't know how to hold the pencil or anything. But by the end of the year, they could read for themselves. I worked hard with them. Afterwards I taught mathematics to the fifth and sixth grade students. I really enjoyed that. But then the war broke out in 1967 – we had long, long holidays then. I can't remember how many months we didn't have school.

"It was a very bad time – you know, we had this kind of

hope that Gamal Abdul Nasser, the Egyptian President, that he would win this war. But something happened – like the Israelis attacked all the Egyptian airplanes and we lost the war. It was too much. We were, of course, disappointed because we had hoped to get a Palestinian state, and instead we got this occupation – we were under occupation for over twenty years ..."

The years under Egyptian administration hadn't been without incident. During the 1957 Suez crisis, Gaza came briefly under Israeli control, before being handed back to the Egyptians, but tensions in the Middle East didn't subside. In 1967, Israel learned to its horror that President Nasser of Egypt had established a joint military command with Jordan, threatening to annihilate the Israelis. A number of the other Arab countries around Israel began to establish military pacts with Egypt – in Israel, the terrified Jews began preparing for full-scale war; but the hostilities were over almost before they had begun. On 5th June 1967, the Israeli airforce attacked all seventeen Egyptian air bases, destroying almost the entire Egyptian air fleet. Without a viable airforce, the Egyptian ground troops were ineffective.

By the end of what came to be known as the Six-Day war, Israel had gained control of the West Bank and Gaza Strip. The Palestinians were now under Israeli occupation. Interestingly, in taking the Palestinian territories, the Israelis inadvertently united the Palestinians who had been split under Jordanian and Egyptian rule. From now on, the yearning to recreate a Palestinian identity would become an ever-increasing force throughout the West Bank and Gaza Strip.

This desire was fuelled by the hatred that the Palestinians felt towards their occupiers. Some say that conditions for the Palestinians improved under the Israelis, but Selwa's view was otherwise. "Since 1967 until the Palestinian State, the Israelis did nothing for Gaza," was her comment. "They never put money in to fix Gaza. There was rubbish and sewage everywhere, and there were not enough medical facilities. It became shameful to go to Gaza."

But for the first time in many years, Gazan and West Bank Palestinians were able to enter Israel to work. The work on offer was for the most part menial, but enabled some of the Gazans to end years of reliance on United Nations subsidies. Then came a new blow – Israel began to construct settlements in the West Bank and Gaza Strip, taking precious land from the Palestinians. Some of the land was sold by Palestinians themselves, but other areas were appropriated by the Israeli authorities. As the number of Israeli settlements increased, so did the resentment of the Palestinians.

In Gaza, the Jewish settlements were located on some of the best agricultural land available and a significant percentage of the region's limited water supply was diverted to them – some of it for maintaining swimming pools and for sprinkling lawns. The Gazans were left with an intermittent supply of inferior quality water – sometimes barely sufficient for their basic needs.

Acts of terrorism towards the occupying Israeli army were countered with harsh punishments and tactics designed to make the Gazans fear their opponents. And as the Gazans began to organize themselves into more defined resistance groups, the day became closer when the tension and bitterness would boil over. The situation was compounded by the 1973 Yom Kippur war. A surprise assault by the Egyptians, under the leadership of President Anwar Sadat on Yom Kippur, the most important Jewish holy day of the year, enabled the Egyptians to retake much of the Sinai desert. Simultaneously, the Syrians broke through into northern Israel, almost as far as Galilee. The shocked Israelis counter attacked, retaking the Golan Heights and crossing the Suez Canal. The Americans intervened and forced a cease-fire before the hostilities could go any further. Once again, the Israelis had staved off their Arab aggressors, but the mistrust and fear engendered amongst them by the hostile behavior of their Arab neighbors enhanced a climate of suspicion that would underpin all of their future dealings with the Palestinians.

It was in 1987 that the situation degenerated beyond control. All through that year, violent incidents between Israelis and Palestinians had become common as the Palestinians felt more and more frustrated with the Israeli occupation and with the increasing indifference of their fellow Arabs to their plight. An incident in early December, in which four men from the Jabalya refugee camp were killed by an Israeli truck driver, was the spark that fuelled the flames. That night, angry demonstrations began in the camp and spread quickly throughout the entire Gaza Strip and West Bank. The Palestinians had begun a movement of resistance against the Israelis – the *intifada*, or "shaking off' – that would last until the early years of the 1990s.

The years of the *intifada* were turbulent ones in world politics too. At the beginning of the *intifada*, world opinion had swung to the side of the Palestinians, supporting their demand for their own state; but in 1991, during the Gulf War, Saddam Hussein began to fire scud missiles at Israel, and once again its citizens took to their bomb shelters. Israel – a tiny country surrounded by Arab nations – received the backing of world opinion. Meanwhile, the Palestinian cause was severely dented by Arafat's support for Saddam Hussein. Against this backdrop, pressure was placed on the Israelis and Palestinians to meet at the negotiating table. The 1993 Oslo accords were born out of a series of secret meetings that took place in Norway – many of the sticking points had been put off to a later date, but crucially, Israel recognized the Palestinian State and a limited autonomy was given to the Palestinians. On 1 July 1994, Yasser Arafat, leader of the Palestinian Liberation Organization set foot in Gaza to take up residence as head of the newly-formed Palestinian Authority. It was a day of mass celebrations all over Gaza and the West Bank. Everywhere, the Palestinian flag – banned under the occupation – now flew freely. But even as the Gazans and West Bankers celebrated, the seeds of discord were being sown. Many Palestinians were distrustful of the new Palestinian Authority and desperately unhappy with the terms of the Oslo Accord.

In the second half of the 1990s, when I visited Gaza, there was an incredible frustration amongst the Gazans about their situation. Israel still retained the power to close off the entire Gaza Strip at will, and the Palestinian Authority had done little to improve life in the refugee camps. One lady we met in Gaza described their squalor to us, at the same time requesting us not to publish her name for fear of reprisals:

"They have some houses now – in the past it was tents only, but now they have improved a little bit. But they still have a roof that isn't concrete, so it may be leaking from the rain. You will find it cramped – two rooms and one bathroom for an average of twenty-five persons living there. Because the families here, when they get married, they have many children, and when the children grow up and want to get married, they live with their parents in the same house. They don't have sewage pipes everywhere in the camps. And the water is disgusting. One of their biggest problems is that they have to use kerosene stoves for cooking, so many people get burns, especially little children."

The economic situation in Gaza at the time of our visit was also very difficult. Our friend gave us an example: "In Gaza, the unemployment is about fifty-five percent at the moment. It is very high. So many Palestinians have to look for work every day in Israel. But, if you want to cross Eretz, you have to be over thirty-five years old, married with children. That way you are less of a security risk. And if your name is recorded on the computer – for throwing stones or whatever – you cannot leave the Gaza Strip."

I asked the lady if she was happy living in Gaza. "I am *Ghazawiyya*, in Arabic that means I am originally from Gaza. But it is very depressing to live here. I see that a third of our land is under Israeli settlement. If anything happens here, any trouble, the Israelis close the borders, it's a siege here; there is no way out for us. We feel like we are in danger. You know, when the Palestinian Authority came here in 1993 we were very, very happy. We wanted peace. We had a big celebration. But now, when you ask the people here, they say this is not real peace. I can't see the peace. Every child should feel this peace. If you can't feel it, what kind of a peace is it?"

I was curious to know what impact the local church was able to make in Gaza. That day, we had the pleasure of visiting friends at the Baptist church there – the only evangelical church in the whole of the Gaza Strip. We had brought in bags full of books – both Christian and secular. The Baptist church had started a little library in order to help provide a service to the impoverished community in Gaza. Many Gazans simply don't have the money to buy any kind of books, and like the West Bank Palestinians, they are always eager to improve their education and take advantage of whatever facilities are available. The Baptist church was dependent on gifts of books from other sources and often it was easier for people to bring books into Gaza than for the church to try and negotiate the complex technical difficulties of importing them.

We sat down with the Christians at the church and asked them about the situation in Gaza. Their replies didn't make for easy listening. A softly-spoken gray-haired man was the first to answer our questions: "Christianity has old roots in Gaza. You can trace the Christian presence back for many, many years. Today there are only about one thousand five hundred Christians in Gaza and we are decreasing in number. Some have left for a better life abroad. Others have converted to Islam for economic reasons. I'll give you an example for our church here: in 1967, about eighty young people attended our youth meetings. Now, there are perhaps only fifteen or so."

As we spoke, I realized just how isolated the Gazan Christians are, surrounded by an overwhelming majority of Muslims. In the seventh century, Arab traders came from the north to Gaza, bringing the new religion of Islam with them. The Gazans wholeheartedly embraced the Muslim faith, and the majority converted to Islam within a very short space of time. Even so, those who chose to keep the Christian faith were allowed to continue their worship without interference. Today, relationships on the whole are good between Christians and Muslims as the two communities have learned how to respect one another.

We visited one or two other friends in Gaza that day, before making our way back to the border. I couldn't help thinking, as a Westerner, how easy it was for me to pass through all these checkpoints. I was desperate to leave the claustrophobic conditions of Gaza behind, and for the first of many times, my heart went out to the Palestinians who were trapped there. When we arrived at the border, it was early evening and a steady stream of workers was pouring back into Gaza from their day's labor in Israel. I was shocked. The Palestinians didn't enter Gaza by the road that we used. Instead, they had to walk through a narrow passageway on the other side of the huge concrete wall. As we wandered along the road to the Israeli checkpoint, we could hear the sound of hundreds of pairs of shuffling feet and the soft murmur of conversation from behind the wall. It was disquieting. The Israeli authorities say that this is a security measure. The Palestinians believe it is designed to dehumanize them. Perhaps both are right.

I left Gaza with a heavy heart. Amongst the Gazans that we had met that day, there was absolutely no sense of optimism about any improvement to conditions there. Life was simply a matter of survival.

Not long afterwards, I shared my thoughts about Gaza with a Jordanian friend, Labib Madanat, Director of the Jerusalem-based Palestinian Bible Society. He understood my reaction completely: "The first time I came to Gaza," Labib told me, "I hated it. I felt so heavy in my heart. I just hated the place. I couldn't wait to leave and as soon as I was back in Israel again, I felt free. You know, the reality of Gaza is that it's a big prison. The people are free within this prison, but ..." he shrugged his shoulders, "... it's a place where difficult things are normal. Remember, many of the people here are not allowed to cross the borders from Gaza to the outside world."

What impressed me was that Labib didn't leave it there.

Even though, as a Jordanian Arab, he often encountered problems at the Gaza checkpoints, he returned time and again to see what the Bible Society could do to help the tiny, isolated community of Christians living in the Gaza Strip. In March 1999, two years after my first visit to Gaza, I found myself returning with Labib and a group of Christians from all over the world for the opening of the Bible Society bookshop in the Gaza Strip. Labib's dreams of helping the people in Gaza had become reality.

Two days before the opening, I drove down to Gaza with Labib and a few friends to look at the bookshop. I was struck by the attention that had been paid to make the interior look bright and attractive. In a place as desolate as Gaza, even this made a real impression. Upstairs, the children's section housed Bible storybooks on colorful red and yellow shelves. Small tables and chairs gave plenty of room for the children to sit and browse. In a corner, a computer and small section of technical and academic books provided a much-needed Internet access-point and resource center for the Gazans.

We sat down to talk; Labib's long legs sticking out at all angles on the tiny children's chair. I asked him what had changed his mind about Gaza and why he had returned. Labib smiled, "The breakthrough for me was when I came to Gaza with Brother Andrew, the founder of Open Doors. We met with some people in Gaza – not Christians. I don't know how, but I just began to see them with different eyes. I fell in love with Gaza and the people here. And right away, we started to think, what can we do for them?"

Labib's desire to help the people of Gaza was fuelled by the increasing number of letters received by the Bible Society from Palestinian Muslims living all over the West Bank – and particularly in the Gaza Strip. Many requested a copy of the Bible. Others wanted to know more about Jesus and how they could meet with Christians. Each reply had to be handled sensitively – in some strict Muslim families, a member who converts to Christianity may be cut off from the family. In extreme cases, the family members might regard it as their duty to kill the apostate. Labib thrust a translation of one of the letters under my nose, so that I could see the interest in the gospel for myself:

21 December 1997

"To the brothers and friends at the Bible Society ... I was hoping, on this joyful occasion (Christmas), to celebrate together this festival – which is precious to my heart and to all our hearts – at the Nativity Church. But, unfortunately, the unbearable conditions which I and other young men are suffering from in Gaza have prevented me from achieving this dream which I always wished and still wishing ... This is not all what I am suffering from here ... I do not even have a friend who can help me through these trying trials which I cannot overcome by myself. I need, therefore, if pos- sible, your help to find someone in Gaza who can help me and teach me how to live and practice the Christian life. You know very well that what I am passing through is very hard and energy-consuming. On my own, I will not be able to overcome these difficulties since my family are Muslim and I am living in a Muslim community. I need a lot, a lot of guidance and understanding."

Labib's plan, a bookshop selling Bibles and Christian books in the heart of Gaza itself, would help the many people in the Gaza Strip who, out of sheer desperation at their circumstances, were looking to Christianity for answers they couldn't find anywhere else. The bookshop would stock secular as well as Christian books, in order to provide a wider service for the Gazan people, but Labib wanted to be open about the Christian emphasis of the shop:

"The shop is on a main street, on a main square of Gaza City. It is there, accessible, clear in front of everybody. Everybody can come into the shop. We are not hiding it – and we intended it to be like that. Jesus was never hiding away from the Romans and from the Jews in some secret place – he was out there in the streets, visible, available for the people, and this shop – the Teacher's Bookshop – should be just like its Master: on the main street. Very much part of the daily life of people passing through. The Muslim majority in Gaza needs to see that the Bible is okay – that they can come freely into this shop and read all kinds of Christian books."

For me, one of the most exciting things about the bookshop was how readily it was accepted and welcomed by the local community. Over the past few years in Gaza, there has been a marked increase in support for Hamas, the fundamentalist Islamic group. But local Muslim leaders have approved the project, and even in the weeks leading up to the opening of the bookshop, a number of people were already calling by, asking if they could get hold of a Bible.

I asked Labib if he and his colleagues had faced any difficulties along the way. "Setbacks?" he replied, laughing. "It's been a wild process. It's been almost four or five years since we first talked about it and even up until now – two days before the opening – we've only just had the electricity connected and suddenly the water supply has stopped! I am sure that Satan wants to rob us of the joy of this accomplishment. We have gone through a long process of all kinds of tape: red, green, blue, orange. But you know, this is not just any bookshop in Gaza. This is not just any Christian bookshop. This is a special bookshop in a very special place. For the first time ever in the history of the Gaza Strip there is a Christian bookshop here. I really want to encourage other Christians to give a bit of prayer for us. You know, here we are – we've finally made it, and that's special indeed!"

As I spoke at length with Labib, I realized how much the bookshop meant to him. He saw it as an answer to the hatred, bitterness and fighting that engulfs this part of the world. Labib – and many Christians like him – do all they can to show God's love and God's message of forgiveness to this troubled society. On his trips to the Gaza Strip, despite the hostility and deliberate provocation sometimes encountered from the Israeli soldiers, Labib and his colleagues made a point of carrying Hebrew Bibles in the car, and they would try and turn situations of potential conflict into an opportunity to share God's love. "But I didn't always succeed," he told me. "Please don't make me into something special. There are other times when I have deliberately humiliated Israelis. I remember once I did so when I was going through customs at the airport ... It's hard to keep on loving. But you know there was a big challenge in all of this. Whenever there were bus bombs or suicide attacks in Israel by Muslim fundamentalists – every time this happened, and I remember very well when I was living on the Jaffa Road in Jerusalem, twice I heard the blast of a bus blowing up – I knew at once what it was. Immediately, it was as if there was a wild cry from Satan saying, 'This is my solution: what about you? What do you have to offer?' And I believe what we have brought to Gaza, this message here, the message of love, of justice, of forgiveness, is God's answer."

On the opening day of the bookshop, we celebrated in Gaza. I have just looked again at the photographs we took. They show a sea of smiling faces; amongst them Labib, Brother Andrew, Bishara and many other Christians – including Messianic Jews – from around the world who had traveled with us from Jerusalem by coach. Sadly there is one face missing from the crowd. Nashat, a young Palestinian, who works closely with Labib at the Bible Society in Jerusalem and had been involved with the Gaza bookshop project. At the last minute, the Israeli authorities refused him permission to come with us to Gaza. As I climbed aboard the bus in Jerusalem, shivering in the chilly dawn, I caught sight of Nashat standing by the roadside, his disappointed face in sharp contrast to the smiles of everybody else around. He had come to wave us off, and smiled bravely as the coach pulled away. To me, it was just one more example of how innocent people suffer in so many different ways in this part of the world.

All the same, it was fantastic to be a witness to the opening of the bookshop in Gaza. It felt like a sign that God hadn't given up on a struggling people whose plight is ignored by so many. As our coach drove into Gaza, we were given a police escort – because of the presence of Israeli citizens amongst us. We went along the winding streets, flanked by police cars with sirens blaring and blue lights flashing. Funnily enough, it almost felt as if we were on some triumphal march, showing that God's people can bring His life and hope into a seemingly impossible situation.

Chapter 4

The Seeds That God Has Planted

"What toil we must endure, what fatigue, while we are attempting to climb hills and the summits of mountains! What, that we may ascend to heaven! If you consider the promised reward, what you endure is less. Immortality is given to the one who perseveres; everlasting life is offered; the Lord promises His Kingdom."

(St. Cyprian:
One Hundred & Twenty Wise Sayings
from The Holy Fathers of the Orthodox Church)

In April 2000 I found myself once again headed for the Middle East, but this time my destination was the Sinai Desert. I gazed breathless out of the window as our plane slowly circled the edge of the desert before swooping over the tips of the granite hills and down onto the landing strip at Sharm el Sheikh. The setting sun caused the entire landscape to blush a gentle mauve before the deepening dusk began to creep around us like an almost tangible mist of soft darkness.

I climbed out of the plane into the muggy heat, almost in a daze, only to be sharply brought to my senses by the clamor and chaos of the terminal. It was most curious – I felt as if I had come home: the indifference of the customs officers, the dark eyes and impossibly long lashes of the Egyptian men, the porters grabbing at my luggage and

demanding a *baksheesh* (tip), the crowds of entire extended
families all of whom turned out to meet loved ones off the
plane, the sheer hubbub of so many people all trying to
speak at the same time all seemed so familiar to me – I'd
forgotten how much I loved the Middle East.

I located my group and dragged my luggage to a jeep
waiting just outside the terminal. Young men threw our
bags up to a Bedouin standing on the roof of the vehicle,
his traditional Arabic *jellabya* robes streaming behind him
in the warm evening breeze. We climbed inside and began
the long drive into the heart of the desert. Night had set in,
and we only saw tantalizing glimpses of scenery caught in
our headlights. Then as the moon came out, rocks and
boulders slowly materialized alongside the road. Our path
wound upwards, climbing through valleys where we could
just about discern steep-sided mountains, washed out and
insipid in the pale moonlight. Finally we slowed down, and
pulled off the road into the desert, the jeep's wheels
spinning in the soft sand. There was no discernible track,
but the drivers knew the route they were taking and soon
enough we found ourselves at the foot of a small *wadi*
where a welcoming fire blazed in front of a Bedouin tent.

After a quick meal of chicken and rice washed down with
a large mug of tea, we unraveled our sleeping bags and lay
down in the *wadi*, just far enough away from the small
bushes, where snakes lurked in the undergrowth. I lay
cocooned in my sleeping bag on the soft sand, wondering
at how entirely comfortable it was, and how very pleasant it
felt looking up at the bright stars pinpricking the darkness,
which, like a soft velvet blanket, wrapped me up as I drifted
off to sleep.

For five days, I joined a group of travelers riding camels
with the Bedouin in the Sinai desert, wandering through
scenery as varied as it was amazing. Once we tracked along
an ever-narrowing ravine, and dismounted at the end,
following a steep zigzagging path up an almost sheer
wall of sand. I slipped and shuffled as the tiny grains of
sand constantly gave way beneath my feet, until I learned

the knack of walking in the compacted footsteps of the person in front. Every time I thought we had reached the summit, another peak appeared high above our heads. We stopped constantly for rests and to drink the tepid water from our flasks. In the desert, the most powerful enemy is dehydration.

Three more rest stops and our climb was at an end. I walked around a rock and found the most breathtaking view spread out in front of us. It looked as if we were standing at the edge of a vast sea of sand, punctuated with spiky thorn bushes and the tips of granite and sandstone mountains just visible in the far distance. Above our heads, a few wisps of cloud echoed the wind waves in the sand at our feet. I felt as if I were standing on top of the whole world.

Just six months later, I returned to the Sinai under very different circumstances. Shortly before, I had received an invitation from Salim Munayer, director of Musalaha, the Israeli/Palestinian Christian reconciliation organization. I asked him what the invitation was all about. "We're planning a trip to the Sinai desert, this time for church leaders from both sides, Arab and Israeli. Are you and Sian willing to come? We'd like to have you here with us. We're celebrating ten years of Musalaha."

I leapt at the chance; I had wanted to do this for years.

I thought back to the first time I had met Salim at the Bethlehem Bible College, where he is the Academic Dean. I was sitting eating lunch in the big basement dining room with the students, when a forty-three year old bundle of energy strode into the room, his eyes casting around and taking in the scene at a glance. Salim moved from person to person talking, joking, his eyes twinkling – then suddenly serious, a sympathetic hand on someone's shoulder saying more than words could.

Eventually he came and sat down at our table to talk with us. At first it was hard work to pin Salim down – I wanted to know more about Musalaha and his own background, but doing so necessitated following several different story-lines at once as he jumped from one subject to another. What soon became clear was that this stocky, curly-haired Palestinian had a unique and fascinating story to tell.

"I was born in the town of Lod, near Tel Aviv," Salim explained. "My family are Palestinian Arabs, but we have Israeli citizenship, which gives us more privileges than many of the Palestinians who live in the West Bank and Gaza. I can travel freely about Israel and the West Bank, without having to apply for permits. That's a great help in my work."

Although Salim's family were from a Greek Orthodox background, he was sent to a Jewish secondary school and began to attend a Bible study group consisting of Jewish and Arab students where he made a commitment to Christ. "You know it's funny, there I was, a Palestinian, helping to plant Messianic Jewish congregations! I would say that in some ways, my faith at that time really drew from a Messianic context. I had never really encountered many Palestinian Christians," he told me.

Salim studied at Fuller Theological Seminary in the States and then returned to Israel, where he found himself working with both Palestinian Christians and Messianic Jewish believers.

"I had a part-time job teaching at Bethlehem Bible College and for the first time I was exposed to the situation of Palestinian Christians. I taught in Arabic and found myself facing the challenge of having to 'invent' theological words in this language. I began to see the struggle facing my own people. The students asked for my advice, such as how to deal with the animosity from their school friends and neighbors when they refused to join in throwing stones at the Israelis. As Christians, they didn't want to use violence, but as Palestinians, they wanted to know how to show sympathy for their own people.

"I also helped to direct a Hebrew training program in Jaffa, teaching leadership training to young Messianic believers. Here too, the students faced their own unique struggles, trying to find their identity as Jews and now as Christians after having accepted Jesus as the Messiah."

The dual nature of Salim's working life graphically illustrated to him the chasm that existed between Palestinian Christians and Messianic Jews. "Here I was teaching these two groups of believers – they both knew Jesus as their Savior, but they were living in two completely different worlds. Most of them had never even met a Christian from the other side."

And so Musalaha was born. The organization, which takes its name from the Arabic word meaning "reconciliation" came into being in 1989, right in the middle of the first *intifada*.

Salim's vision was to try and bring Messianic Jews and Palestinian Christians face to face, so that they could begin to talk to one another and break down the barriers that divided them. "There were so many injustices taking place and so much theological speculation, I came to the conclusion that the best theology to deal with this situation was reconciliation. More than anything, believers from both sides needed to talk. So much propaganda, so much dehumanization was going on. They needed to see what they had in common, not what separated them. In this way, perhaps we could begin to bring about changes in their lives and in our societies," he recalled.

Salim was joined early on by his good friend, Evan Thomas, a burly New Zealander who leads a Messianic Jewish congregation in Netanya, a small coastal town just north of Tel Aviv. God was moving in Evan's life too. At that time, he had just got to know a small group of Palestinian Christians, a first for him, as he explained to a friend of mine:

"Our congregation had planned an evangelistic campaign in Haifa. To our surprise, fifteen Palestinian Christians appeared on the first day, offering their help. During those three days, I found it an incredible experience to work with the Palestinian Christians, especially as things were really heating up towards the *intifada* and they'd made this specific decision to take the gospel out among their Jewish neighbors. As a result of our campaign, eight Israelis prayed to receive Jesus as the Messiah – seven of them were led to the Lord by the Palestinian Christians! By that time, God had my attention. I began to realize that I had some brothers and sisters out there who were Arab Palestinians. As an immigrant from New Zealand, I didn't really have much of an upbringing of intolerance towards them, but I was very aware that there was this 'them and us' concept. As a combat soldier, I knew that there would be times that I would have to serve in a situation where they could well be my enemy. My community certainly told me that they were my enemy. Suddenly I had to deal with this dichotomy – here in front of me was my brother, my enemy. And I understood that God was speaking to me . . ."

Evan and Salim worked on a format that would enable them to bring Messianic Jews and Palestinian Christians together. One of the main problems facing them was the challenge of finding a suitable venue.

"Imagine," said Salim in his rapid-fire manner, "a Palestinian teenager who has lived through the *intifada* and has seen his father shot dead in front of his eyes. Now, take an Israeli boy whose sister has been the victim of a suicide bomb attack. How are you going to bring those two young people to a place where they can talk – *really* talk? If you put them in a room together, they will end up screaming at each other. So, we chose the desert. You see the desert is a neutral place. It is not a Jewish or an Arab place. It is non-territorial. In the Bible it is used as a test of faith. That is where Jesus and the prophets went to pray. If you don't co-operate and help each other, you can't survive there. It is a place where you see you are small and God is big."

In my mind's eye I could see myself sitting on a sandy plateau writing up my diary after a day in the saddle on my Sinai trip. We had spent the day riding through the mountains, our surefooted camels picking their way through the loose shingle. In the morning, we passed by a huge stony outcrop which is known as the Rock of Inscriptions. Here, ancient travelers would inscribe their names, signs or messages to show that they had passed through. On one side I could make out some ancient pictures of camels and gazelles. On the other was the inscription of a Jewish menorah with a cross in the middle made by an early Jewish convert to Christianity.

Salim was right. The desert is a place where you feel very small. I was so conscious of my dependency on my Bedouin fellow travelers. They knew the best places to camp for the night, and they walked in the rhythm of the desert – stopping for two or three hours at lunch time to sleep and conserve their energy in the middle of the day, always talking softly as sound carries clearly across the sandy plains. We rode in the mornings and afternoons, our heads and faces shrouded in scarves to keep away the worst of the sun's rays. It had the effect of reducing us to vague muffled figures, our features subsumed by the loose garments that we wore. Every day our lives had assumed the simplicity of desert life – rising with the sun and going to sleep, exhausted, in the early evening when the heavy dusk fell quickly. Our food was basic, and I realized to my surprise that I was relishing life away from the comforts of Western living. Our group had knitted together very quickly, helping one another with the camels, reading stories at lunchtime, sharing medical supplies. The last night of our holiday was spent in a hotel in Sharm el Sheikh, and I had been taken aback when everybody resumed their "normal" clothes. Suddenly our identities re-emerged and the group, no longer interdependent, broke up into little clusters. I could see from my own experience the wisdom of Salim's choice of venue.

His first step was to find a contact who would be willing to take a group of mixed Arabs and Israelis into the desert. Not everybody was open to the kind of work that Salim and Evan wanted to do and they had to scout around to find people to help. Over the following years, they developed a format for these desert encounters which provide a safe place for these young people to begin to open up to one another – and to God. Salim gave me more details:

"What do we do with the young people? They load camels, share water, cook, hike. They learn from places of historical interest. It is like stripping you naked and who you are comes across very clearly. They have fun and are challenged together. Slowly people get to know each other. The conversations start to change to become, 'I didn't know your people were suffering so much ...' The language is moving towards confession and repentance. On each camel, we put a Jew and a Palestinian. We discovered it's not the same if we use jeeps and Land Rovers. Their engines are loud and the kids end up shouting and making a lot of noise. But a camel has a quiet rhythm of walking. They are amazing animals – they can carry up to a quarter of a ton, will never step on a human, and can go for weeks on end without water. The atmosphere makes people quiet. Then they start listening to others. We can provide an atmosphere where they can listen to each other. That's what Jesus did with his disciples. Walking and talking. People find they can talk about the most painful things without ending up shouting at each other.

"One thing – I think it is difficult perhaps for you to grasp just how deep the layers of pain and animosity go," Salim told me. "By the age of five, children here have a very clear idea of who the enemy is. Subconsciously it is there."

"But do the desert encounters really work?" I asked him. In answer, he showed me part of a diary written by a counselor on one of their desert trips:

"Thursday morning our journey began. We left behind air conditioning, cold water, TV, the comforts of home and our peer groups. We stepped out into a dry, yet rich wilderness that had a very different experience to offer us. I was struck that the moments where our group was most integrated and well balanced was when we were moving. Most started out with a partner or in groups of three, mixed Arab and Israeli, one leading the camel, one riding and the other walking alongside, switching periodically. At each rest stop, the people would change places and these partnerships shuffled around and suddenly mixed. When a new person began leading your camel down narrow trails, you quickly became friends with this stranger who determined exactly where and how fast you would go ... The next day, we continued on through what was probably the most difficult climb of the trip, coaxing our reluctant camels to carry our friends and our gear up a rather steep mountain. Some camels groaned and stopped every few steps. It was an exercise in cooperation and reconciliation just trying to get this burdened animal up the mountain. Until the second evening, the spiritual dimension of our desert encounter had fallen second to noise and activity. Yet it seems that God used the games, songs and even camels to mould us into a group, not simply a collection of Palestinian and Jewish participants, but a group of people who were ready to worship Him and to listen to His word. That night, waiting for our dinner by the light of oil lamps, the Holy Spirit moved in a very simple and true way. We began by sharing songs in English, Arabic and Hebrew. Then one of the leaders shared about the young people in the Bible, and how each of them, like Joseph, had listened to the voice of God. One girl then said, 'It is important for me to be together like this, with Arabs and Jews. I am so glad that we are here.' Another young man agreed, 'We are joined by faith in Jesus our Messiah.' "

The diary entry left me with a thirst to know more details. I asked Salim if he could give me an example of somebody who had been profoundly affected by a Musalaha trip. His eyes lit up, "Yes of course, for instance there is a young Palestinian man, 'Samir', whose father was killed by the Israeli army. He was full of hatred and revenge, even to the point of seeking a way to get even with the other side. After a few months of discussion with us, he agreed to come on a desert trip. I was kind of afraid a little bit – how he would react to the Jewish side, to the Israelis who had served in the army. And now they were stuck in the desert together for five days!

"On the first day he was very quiet; he didn't say anything, he was just there. Then, in the evening we divided into small groups, and we asked a Jewish person and a Palestinian person to sit together and talk. It just happened that Samir sat with a Jewish man that had lost all his family in the Holocaust. So they began to talk about what it means to be lost. That was one step, but it wasn't enough."

A short time after the group returned from the desert trip, Salim took them to the place where Samir's father had been shot. Samir was asked to describe the shooting and the effect that it had on him – then the group prayed for him. Afterwards, they traveled to Ben Yehuda Street in Jerusalem, where a suicide attack had recently taken place. "Esther", an Israeli girl from the group, who had been standing on the street minutes before the bomb exploded, told the others how the incident had affected her. She still suffered intense psychological trauma from the experience.

Salim described Samir's reaction to Esther's experiences: "Afterwards, we walked up the road together and Samir said to me, 'You know, many times I wanted to be like one of the suicide people. Because of what they did to me – to my people, to my family. All the loss. But now I am gaining back who I am, my identity. The violence is going ...'"

Just recently, I watched the video of a documentary made by the Dutch evangelical broadcasting company, Evangelische Omroep (EO). Part of the documentary traces the experiences of Samir and Esther. At one point, Samir described the day his father was killed:

"My father was very active during the *intifada*. There was a demonstration for peace because somebody had been killed in Beit Sahour and he joined in. A boy started to swear at the soldiers and when the boy started to throw stones, they shot back with tear gas. They beat up the demonstrators and there was quite a fight. Everybody ran away ... A group of soldiers came from up the hill and when they saw my father they fired at him. He fell to the ground and said that he surrendered, but they didn't take that seriously. They fired again twice at his back and he died – a dum-dum bullet tore up his liver. That's how he died. He stayed on the ground for about forty minutes – no one dared to help him ... An ambulance came that took him, but before he was taken to the hospital he was interrogated first about the demonstration. He was treated from eleven o'clock in the morning until nine in the evening. At 9.30pm he died. The day my father died a woman hit me four times. She said that I had to cry but I was just laughing because it was such a big shock for me ... I don't cry easily. I suffered a great loss. I was not the only one, but I needed my dad very much at that time. He was both my father and my friend. Just imagine that you lose someone whom you really love, that hurts terribly and then it's easy to start hating the Jewish people. I wanted to join something and that's why I joined a political party. I became very active during the *intifada*. I tried to find revenge ... "

Esther then recounted her story: "I had just come into my office which is on top of Ben Yehuda ... and as soon as I walked in the explosions happened ... I saw people every-where and people carrying people and I felt, well should I go down? But by this time the ambulances were here and I thought now it's just going to be more of a mess. To be honest, what was concerning me the whole time was my friend, because we had gone out to lunch together and split up to do two different things and come back and I got back, but she hadn't returned yet. For four hours we didn't hear anything from her and we called all the hospitals to try and find her and no one knew anything. They were taking all the details that had to do with how she looked or if she had any scars or any marks on her that we could recognize and that was very, very hard. I was very scared that she could be one of the people lying down below. Later, when I got home, I heard from her and she was okay. It hit me how close I myself had been and I was very much in shock. I didn't know what to do with the whole thing ... "

When Esther shared her story with Samir, she had a very clear agenda: "I wanted him at first to know that it has not caused me to hate him or his people – that I knew that the majority of the Palestinians do not agree with killing. I wanted him to see that, as much as I had experienced it and had to deal with it all, and it wasn't easy and people lost their loved ones and that could easily bring a person to hate, I did not want to go that way. And God had to deal with me, but He did and I wanted Samir to see that – that I still loved him and his people."

Samir's final comment is a testimony to God's work in his heart: "I've been changed in many ways. I don't think any more about revenge. But I am still interested in politics. Musalaha has had a great influence on me. It has given me back my humanity."

Reconciliation is a process, a long and difficult journey. I remember Cindy telling me how God had challenged her to love the Arabs: "I got to the place where I began to feel less hostility towards Arab Christians. After all, they are my brothers and sisters in Christ. But to love a *Muslim* Arab! That seemed so difficult. It was only step by step that God changed my heart, and showed me the extent of the prejudices buried deep beneath."

Salim and Evan recognize the importance of this process. Once the group has taken the step of meeting together in the desert – and there are those who can't even bring themselves to go that far – they are then encouraged to move forwards. The new relationships and attitudes, which have been gently nurtured in the desert, now need to grow within the context of their daily lives.

One follow-up group visited two of the most evocative settings in which you could ever ask Palestinians and Israelis to meet. They drove to Deir Yassin, a little village located to the west of Jerusalem. In 1948 the village was attacked by Jewish militant groups who killed and mutilated men, women and children. Well over a hundred Palestinians were murdered in the village that day. The Deir Yassin massacre is engraved on the heart and mind of every Palestinian. Salim explained the details, "In some areas during the fighting in 1948, when the Jewish militant groups approached other Palestinian villages, they told the people, 'You had better leave the village or we do to you, what we did in Deir Yassin'. Many of the Israelis learn in history that in 1948 the Arabs just ran away of their own accord, leaving empty villages behind. That is a myth."

Next, the group visited Yad Vashem, the Jewish Holo- caust museum which, ironically, is located on the other side of the same hilltop as Deir Yassin. Here the Palestinians were shown the extent of the atrocities committed against the Jews during the Holocaust, and the graphic reasons why they so desperately needed a homeland of their own. One of the group members, a Messianic Jewish pastor called Asher searched through the records for his own family and made some grim discoveries concerning his relatives who had perished in the concentration camps. He too was interviewed on the EO broadcast, and spoke about his visit to Yad Vashem that day: "My Grandfather escaped from Europe and came to the US. Most of his brothers and sisters were killed in Europe. Why? What did I do to be lucky? How did it happen that I was able to be born? It sort of feels like the question 'why?' The other question is 'who?' Who are we? Where did I come from? My name, Asher, comes from my Great Grandfather. My son is called after my Grandfather. It's a sense of understanding who you are ... part of you wants to identify with the Holocaust and part of you wants to get away from it. Part of me wants to say, 'That's not my name, that's not me'. And part of me wants to preserve it."

Asher has been involved with Musalaha trips and is deeply challenged by the whole process of learning to listen to the other side: "If you want to be reconciled with someone else, you need to hear what is hurting them and not try to just convince them of what you want, even if you are right," he commented. "I'm a Zionist. I moved my family here for Zionist reasons. My life here is based on the fact of the prophecies and the covenant that said our people have a right to live here and I moved my whole family here at great hardship. Other brothers and sisters in Christ say that's almost meaningless to them. That's a difficult thing. It makes it so that almost everything that you stand for – ideologically, prophetically, theologically – your whole motivation comes up in front of a contradiction of everything that they stand for. And that becomes a test of love. Does your love become stronger than prophecy? I'm a Bible teacher. I still think I'm right in terms of our interpretation of Scripture and yet I have a greater mandate from the Bible to love. Love, as I understand it in 1 Corinthians 13 is a greater commandment than the prophetic agenda ... the mandate to love them and to bring justice is stronger to me than those political things and prophetic interpretations, so I'm finding in myself a place of integrity. I have to put my theological interpretations a little bit on the back burner and deal with the immediate mandate, which is to love these people and to do what I can to help them."

I expected to learn that working for Musalaha takes its toll on Salim, Evan and the other staff too, but I was surprised by the extent of the difficulties that they face. Salim has received death threats in the past and both he and Evan constantly run the risk of being misunderstood by people from their own communities. Evan expanded the situation, "For Salim, it seems that he's in a position where both sides can extremely mistrust him. Well, he had an Israeli upbringing you see, and so there is this suspicion – he didn't grow up in the West Bank, but in Lod, which is Israeli territory. They rejected him for what they saw as his Palestinian bias. That's what makes him – is making him – into a bridge person. That's what's making me into a bridge person, because of who we are and our circumstances. Myself as an immigrant, apolitical even in my thinking, gives me that opportunity. Pastoring, for many years, a local congregation so diverse and full of immigrants, dealing with the various intolerances here. These are things that create you into bridge people, which is what you have to be. But, bridge people get walked on, that's part of the price. Both of us have fairly broad shoulders, we can be a little feisty in nature, which means we're thick-skinned, we can take it. And we care for one another, Salim and I. We watch over one another, we're nearly every day on the telephone."

Added to the personal pressures are the frustrations stemming from the sheer complex logistics of organizing any kind of meeting between Palestinians and Israelis. "Let me give you an example," said Salim. "During the Passover in April, I am taking a group that we call 'Post Army – Post *Intifada*': Israelis who have completed their military service and Palestinians that grew up during the *intifada* – we want to bring them together for a Sinai desert experience for five days. The Israelis don't have a problem to get a visa to go to Sinai, but to take the Palestinians I have to get a visa from Egypt. The Palestinians aren't allowed to cross certain borders, so they have to cross from Rafah, at the bottom of the Gaza Strip. This means we have two groups crossing the border at different points. And not only do we have to get permission from the Egyptians for the Palestinians to go to Sinai, we also have to get permission from the Israeli army for the Palestinians to cross Israel to get to the Gaza Strip."

I wondered what the personal demands were on a Christian in this part of the world who chooses to walk the path of reconciliation and forgiveness. During my travels, I had often been stretched by the whole process of meeting believers from either side. Quite apart from the emotional roller coaster ride of listening to their often tragic stories, there was also the need to remain objective and resist the anger that welled up inside me towards the extremists of both nationalities. Evan is frank about the price that he personally has to pay, "It has been a major learning curve for me to enter into that place where I have to feel – I'm literally forced to feel – empathy for another brother's community where there is such incredible emotional demand. You know, every crisis here brings you to that place. But in the midst of that, it seems that you get stretched that little bit extra, and so when there is an atrocity or a crisis in the West Bank or in one of the Arab congregations I'm aware of, they're my brothers. It's one of my own. I can pick up the phone and go over and visit, spend the weekend. I can have that genuine heart-interest, and the Lord makes room for it, so I'm pushed beyond the walls of my own cultural interests."

I never got to meet Evan Thomas – his side of the story was told to a friend of mine on another occasion. Evan traveled to the desert with the Musalaha group in October 2000, where I hoped very much to spend some time talking with him, but I was caught in the West Bank in the middle of the rioting that was to herald the new *intifada*. It was only later that month, when I finally made it to the Musalaha offices in West Jerusalem that Salim and the other staff told me what a success that trip had been. Many Israeli and Palestinian pastors had been given the opportunity to open up to one another at a deep level, allowing pain to be healed, and to commit themselves to supporting each other. Looking back, the timing of the event was highly significant as the fighting began again in earnest and once more, Israelis and Palestinians found themselves embroiled in an endless round of tit-for-tat military incursions and suicide attacks.

Perhaps this new *intifada* is a real test of the depth of Musalaha's work amongst the Christian communities in the Holy Land. A few months into the fighting, I received an email from Salim:

"In spite of the situation, we rejoice that we are able to see the fruits of reconciliation. We recently spoke to a pastor from the Palestinian village of Beit Jala who, along with his family, has been caught in the crossfire between Palestinian and Israeli gunmen. He told us of the efforts of several Jewish believers who have reached out to him and his church: 'After or even during nights of bombardment and shooting, we receive calls from Messianic Jewish friends reminding us of their prayers and love.' One such call came from a Jewish believer whom he had met on a desert trip, 'It was very special to hear from him ... It is so nice to know that we have not been forgotten by our brothers on the other side. Yes, we are Palestinian; yes they are Jews; but a oneness exists.'"

At the same time, Salim told us about a Messianic congregation who had arranged baskets of food and supplies for Palestinian Christians who were suffering financially because the border closures meant they couldn't leave the West Bank to work in Israel. One Jewish believer had even taken the trouble to write little notes in Arabic and put them in each basket, telling the recipients of her love and prayers for them.

It's easy, particularly now, two years later, to look at the reports on the news of yet another major suicide attack and to wonder what difference the work of an organization like Musalaha can really make to such an impossible situation. But God works in the seemingly small things – one changed heart, one healed life is important to Him. And who knows the ripple effect that can have on a community. I remember speaking with a group of elderly Palestinian Christian ladies who had attended a Musalaha women's conference. Their Muslim neighbors were amazed that they wanted to have anything to do with Israeli women – even the Christian ladies themselves were doubtful of how effective the conference would be. But after they had met with the Messianic Jewish women, and discovered that they all shared the same fears and worries about their families and that they could pray for one another, they came back to the West Bank in a very positive frame of mind – that really impressed their neighbors.

The desert follow-up encounters can also be a very powerful tool in speaking to the different communities about God's love. One mixed group of young Palestinians and Israelis stayed in the West Bank, working to clear a blocked water supply in a Palestinian village. The local leaders were astonished that Israelis should want to help them, so the group took the opportunity to explain how God's love goes beyond national identities.

A few weeks ago, I heard about yet another suicide attack, this time in Tel Aviv. I was struck by how sad it is that we so often only hear the negative things that are happening in this part of the world. What of the believers here, whose sacrificial love has profoundly impacted others around them? As I wondered what would come of the latest round of hostilities, I was reminded of a comment made by a participant after she came back from a desert trip with Musalaha:

"What may result in years to come, if the seeds of anger and bitterness begin to grow, they will be choked by the seeds that God has planted here, in these days in the desert. And memories will serve both a Palestinian and a Jew, reminding them of friendships formed, faith shared, and a God who binds His followers together in love."

Chapter 5

The Red Stones

"Because you are my help,
I sing in the shadow of your wings.
My soul clings to you;
your right hand upholds me."
(Psalm 63:7–8)

Ask me to pick up a friend from the airport and I'm as happy as Larry. I'm an avid people-watcher and an airport arrivals-hall provides some of the best opportunities around. On this particular evening in September 2000, I was in my element, scrutinizing the people around me – trying to visualize who they were waiting for and watching a hundred different reunions, wondering about the circumstances of the people involved. I was waiting for a KLM flight from Holland, scanning the scattered groups of people coming through immigration to see if any of them looked remotely Dutch. Judging by the trolleys heaped with luggage, the latest group of arrivals must have come on a transatlantic flight. Then came the Dutch at last – some tall and slender, others shorter and stockier, but most with the unmistakable firm features and blue eyes of people born and bred in the Low Countries.

I spotted Sian as she came walking through the swing doors, anxiously scanning the crowd until she caught sight of me. Her features relaxed in relief and I pulled her trolley under the barrier in front of me, eager to grab a coffee and catch up with her news. We had plenty of time to talk – our plane for Israel didn't take off until early the next morning and we had booked rooms in one of the airport hotels.

I can still remember the precise moment we heard the news. We were sitting at a table in the restaurant, discussing our itinerary and the possibility of spending a few days on a kibbutz, when something on the television screen above our heads caught my attention. I glanced up and realized to my dismay that the newsreader was describing rioting in Jerusalem; that morning Israeli politician, Ariel Sharon, flanked by a thousand armed policemen had walked up to the Temple Mount, the Muslim holy site located just above the Wailing Wall. The Palestinians were incensed at what was a deliberately provocative act. As a result, sporadic rioting had broken out in Jerusalem and already ten Palestinians lay dead in the streets.

My heart ached with sadness for my Palestinian and Israeli friends. Although we didn't know it at the time, things were going to take a rapid turn for the worse. It was almost as if, for the past few years, the deep chasm between the two nations had been papered over and some semblance of normality had returned to the Middle East. Sharon's actions had ripped off the paper-thin covering and exposed the festering wounds that lay underneath. The second *intifada* had just begun.

When we landed at Tel Aviv airport the next afternoon, the atmosphere was relatively relaxed. Crowds of Jews were returning home for Yom Kippur in a holiday mood. Sian was pulled over for questioning, while I breezed through the Israeli checks with the bare minimum of questions: "Shalom. What is the purpose of your visit? Who are you staying with? Where will you be traveling?"

Once the security officers had dispensed with Sian, we made our way through the crowds towards the bus terminal, anxious to get to Jerusalem as soon as possible. It was more than likely that we would face problems traveling into the West Bank where we were staying, and we wanted to get there before night fell if possible. Suddenly, Sian's eyes lit up and she disappeared into the crowd, reemerging a few minutes later with a volunteer worker from the Bethlehem Bible College in tow. Good news, as that was where we were headed. We hitched a lift with the volunteer and asked him about the situation in the West Bank.

"There is trouble at the Bet Lehem border," he told us, shrugging his shoulders. "The soldiers let me out, but I don't know if we can get back in again. Maybe yes, maybe no. I'll try the Beit Jala checkpoint."

Beit Jala is an attractive Palestinian village located just to the west of Bethlehem. I remembered the times I'd climbed up the steep hill from Bethlehem, peeking into the pretty courtyard gardens of the cream colored stone houses lining the winding road. Up towards the Israeli checkpoint at the top of the hill, the land falls steeply away to the right, giving a beautiful view across the valley. On the other side stands the Israeli settlement of Gilo, a suburb of Jerusalem built on land appropriated from the Palestinians. Just beyond the checkpoints on the crest of the hill lie the playgrounds and low buildings of the Hope School, where Bishara and Selwa worked when they first returned to the West Bank.

A friend of ours, Zaki, lives just opposite the Hope School, in a typical flat-roofed house with his mother, brother, sister-in-law and nephews. The last time we visited the family, we climbed up to a little room built on top of the roof where Zaki has his studio. Lying on the workbench was a group of beautifully executed Bible scenes painted in oils on small pieces of deep-grained olive wood. He offered us one of the paintings each. I chose a picture of a shepherd standing underneath a tree, a sheep tucked under his arm. Sian pulled out a package from her bag and handed it to Zaki. Inside was a bottle of linseed oil and other materials for his painting. He was overjoyed – it was almost impossible to get hold of things like these in the West Bank.

Zaki's mother appeared with tea and huge bunches of grapes from their vines. We sat outside on the roof listening politely as she tried to persuade one of us to buy the house opposite them, which had recently come up for sale. "Please, buy the house – it's cheap for you," she put her hand on my arm. "Then we know we will have good neighbors. It's beautiful here isn't it? You would like it so much, I promise you."

I agreed with her. The houses in this street were spacious and the sloping gardens behind them were luxuriant with their citrus trees, olive groves, vines and beautiful flowers. But there was one major drawback: the slopes of Beit Jala provide an excellent vantage point for Palestinian militants and some of the settlers in Gilo to fire across the valley at one another. If there is unrest in the West Bank, it is very common for fighting to flare up in Beit Jala and the residents have lost count of the number of times the Israeli tanks have rolled into the village. I wasn't sure I wanted to buy a house in the middle of a conflict zone, pretty though it was.

As our minibus turned off the main road from Tel Aviv and pulled up the other side of the hill towards Beit Jala, we peered out of the windows, anxiously scanning the roads for any signs of trouble. Everything seemed under control although the streets were suspiciously empty. We slowed down at the crossroads, turned right and drew up at the Israeli checkpoint. The soldiers stopped us and flicked through our passports, glancing at our faces and then, to our relief, waved us on.

At the Bible College, Bishara was standing in the garden. His greeting was warm, but Bishara was clearly unhappy. "Well my friends, you have chosen an interesting time to come and visit us. Who knows what is going to happen. It's not very good, I'm afraid. But perhaps it will all blow over soon. Let's hope so."

"Have there been any more problems today?" I asked him.

"Today, not so far. But usually if there is a demonstration or fighting, it is in the afternoon. We'll see."

We left our luggage in the newly constructed guest wing, and walked into town to get a feel of the atmosphere. This was a Bethlehem I had never seen before. For the most part, the shops were shuttered with heavy metal grilles and the normally bustling streets were virtually deserted. Here and there, small clusters of people stood talking, their eyes anxious, glancing up every now and then to scan their surroundings. A breeze gusted down the streets, sending the dust swirling along in front of us; something fluttered at my feet. I bent to pick it up. It was a small leaflet, printed with the photograph of a Palestinian boy and some text in Arabic. Sian translated: "This is one of the boys who was killed yesterday. They've given his name and date of birth, and the word *shahid* – 'martyr'."

Back at the Bible College, Bishara explained the closed shops. "They've been ordered to close by the Palestinian Authority as a sign of mourning for yesterday's deaths. It's quite usual for this to happen. Only the shops selling essential goods stay open."

After we had showered, we climbed up onto the flat roof of the Bible College and looked at the view around us. Behind the college, a little valley was spotted with white stone houses, each with its own tiny olive grove where a few goats and chickens scratched around in the dusty red earth. In front of the college sprawled the untidy mass of the al Azza refugee camp – one of several built in Bethlehem to house the 1948 Palestinian refugees. Once, Bishara took us to visit a family who lived in the Deheishah refugee camp, which is located on the outskirts of Bethlehem. We counted at least eight people living in two small breeze-block rooms. Many of the Christians associated with the Bible College work to help these refugees, running summer camps for the children, and inviting Western medical teams over to hold health clinics there. A few years ago, occupants of the Deheishah camp, which has a totally Muslim population, put up a banner at the entrance proclaiming, "We appreciate the work of Bethlehem Bible College."

To one side of the college roof, I could see straight along the Hebron Road, past the greengrocer's shop to Rachel's

Tomb at the far junction. I blinked, hardly believing my eyes. On the left-hand side of the road, near the junction, a gleaming new hotel was in the final stages of construction. Bishara came over to see what we were laughing at, then joined in with us, saying, "They're crazy you know. It's a beautiful hotel – we had my son's wedding reception there recently. But who would build a hotel in that location? They must be mad!"

"Well, it'll be a great spot for the foreign journalists," I replied. "What a close-up view of the fighting!" Located barely two hundred meters from Rachel's Tomb, the building was standing right in the middle of one of Bethlehem's worst flashpoints. I wondered how many guests would be comfortable staying so near to the action.

Halfway along the road, we could see the Palestinian Authority soldiers standing outside their guard post. They had placed a row of red and white metal drums across the road and were turning back cars and pedestrians away from Rachel's Tomb.

"They don't want any trouble," Bishara sounded relieved. "That's good. They're making sure the boys don't go up to the junction and start throwing stones at the soldiers. Maybe they will contain the problems."

At the end of the road, by the Kand Company garage, I saw the rifle butts of the Israeli soldiers gleaming in the sun. It seemed as if nobody was taking any chances.

We spent a very pleasant afternoon reading books and talking on the roof, enjoying the sunshine. Bishara was due to leave in a couple of days to speak at a church conference in Sweden. We were planning to travel out to the Sinai desert the next night to spend time with a Musalaha group before returning to Jerusalem to visit some Messianic Jewish contacts; so we made the most of the time we had left together, catching up on the latest news.

The following morning we repacked our bags, taking only gear we would need for the desert: light trousers and long-sleeved shirts, headscarves, water bottles and stout desert boots. After lunch, we went up to sit on the roof again, but today the atmosphere was tense. Small groups of boys and young men dressed in T-shirts and jeans began wandering past the Bible College towards Rachel's Tomb. A few carried small slings in their hands and one or two had already pulled their T-shirts over their heads, leaving only a small slit for their eyes. It was clear a message had gone out to the community – the Palestinian Authority had no intention of turning them back today and the *shebab* – or young stone-throwers – were out in force. Black smoke already spiraled high into the clear blue sky from a pile of flaming tires at the end of the road and the acrid smell of burning rubber hit our nostrils. It wasn't long before the stone throwing began.

When you travel to the Middle East, it's easy to see why stones are such a favored weapon. The small, sharp rocks are everywhere and quite lethal if they hit their target with any kind of force. During the first *intifada*, it was common for even quite young Palestinian children to throw stones at Israeli cars entering their territory, as a sign of their anger and frustration. The older boys targeted the Israeli soldiers, aware of the inadequacy of their weapons against the sophisticated firearms of the occupying forces. But many had reached the point where they could no longer stand by and do nothing.

At the junction by Rachel's Tomb, the Palestinian boys had built themselves a makeshift barricade. The majority of them were tucked into the alleys and doorways further down the road, out of reach of the soldier's bullets, but a few, more daring youngsters ran up behind the barricade, hurling stones and molotov cocktails at the Israeli troops stationed at the other side of the junction. We could hear the answering crack of rifle shots as they fired back. Then suddenly a deep boom sounded and we all jumped. The boys ran back from the flashpoint, T-shirts over their faces. Canisters of tear gas landed in a puff of thin white smoke which drifted back down the road. Our eyes smarted from the fumes, and down in the street below the boys were coughing and wiping their eyes with their hands.

The skirmishes began to take on a rhythmic pattern: slowly the Palestinian boys advanced up to the barricade, throwing stones and bottles as they went. We could hear the smash of glass and the ring of stone on metal from where we stood. Then the soldiers retaliated with bullets and tear gas, driving the boys back down the road again and again. I watched, mesmerized by the strange ritual.

At first it seemed almost harmless, then suddenly a loud cry of *"Allahu Akhbar"* went up from the boys at the junction, quickly followed by the wail of a siren. An ambulance that had been waiting in the road below us peeled away from the wall and rushed up the street, the noise of its siren drowning out the cries of the *shebab*. In the distance, the boys manhandled a limp body, waiting to lift it into the back of the ambulance.

All that afternoon, the *shebab* played their deadly game of cat and mouse with the soldiers while we sat drinking tea on the roof and watching. I could barely take in what was happening – the whole scenario seemed unreal. People were being wounded and killed in front of my eyes and there was nothing I could do to stop it.

Every now and then, a fresh group of youngsters would arrive on the scene, just as others left to go home, their arms around their friends' shoulders. I was amazed at how young they were. It was noticeable that the boys involved in the actual fighting were teenagers or even younger. The older men, more likely to have families to support, stayed well back beyond range.

Some say that young boys are deliberately encouraged to go to the front line – that the death of a child of only ten or eleven adds fuel to the Palestinian media machine. I tried to work out what was going on today. Was it just a controlled way of releasing tension? Or did they want another young martyr for their own publicity? Or, were they just totally frustrated at their sheer inability to do anything about the situation they found themselves in? You just never know what is going on behind the scenes.

Suddenly there was another huge boom from the junction

and the sirens began their eerie wailing again. For the young Palestinians the fighting was a matter of honor. The wounded were treated like heroes. Those who died became martyrs and their families were given financial compensation by the Palestinian Authority. It is said that some of the boys will pick a favorite photograph of themselves and carry it in their back pocket when they join the demonstrations, so that if they are killed, that particular photograph will appear on the printed martyr's leaflet.

The Muslim culture feeds this situation too. According to the Islamic faith, if you die a martyr you are transported directly to heaven, into the lap of luxury, where the men are cared for by a harem of beautiful young virgins. The only other way to heaven is to earn it by good deeds. You can see the appeal for these idealistic, frustrated young boys, many of whom have little to look forward to in this life. Nowadays though it is thought that Islam plays a smaller role than it did in the past. Many of the suicide bombers who have attacked since the beginning of the second *intifada* have far less affiliation to extremist Islamic factions. Instead the prevailing motivation is one of utter hopelessness.

I asked Selwa how the Palestinian mothers feel when their boys join in the stone throwing. "Well," she told me, "some of them are proud to have a martyr in the family. Their photograph is everywhere and their memory is honored. But others definitely not. They are completely upset."

I thought of the family we had visited in the Deheishah camp. One of their sons, Mohammed, was wounded in a confrontation with Israeli soldiers a few years ago, and died as a result of his injuries. The walls of their living room were covered with photographs and pictures of the family martyr. We were introduced to his little nephew, who had been named Mohammed in memory of his uncle. It was clear that Mohammed's name would be honored by this family, but equally obvious that his death was a traumatic and tragic event for them.

Suddenly I remembered we were due to leave Bethlehem that evening, and I went inside to phone Salim to see if we needed to alter our plans. "No, no," he said, "the fighting will be finished by the end of the afternoon. That's how it goes. There's no problem leaving later on. How are the roads? Stones? Broken glass? Yes – then I'll meet you at the border otherwise I'll get a flat tire if I try to drive further."

By early evening, Salim's prediction had come true. The *shebab* had all dispersed and the street was quiet, so we decided to walk along to the border to see if it would be possible to leave by that route later on. The mess was incredible – jagged stones and broken glass lay strewn all over the road, interspersed with empty tear gas canisters, spent bullet cartridges and the occasional home-made sling. I picked up one of the cartridges and examined it – it seemed as if the Israeli soldiers had been using live ammunition and not rubber bullets. No wonder there had been so many casualties. I pocketed a tear gas canister to take home as a souvenir. It still smelled of fumes.

I examined the barricade the Palestinian boys had been using – a few oil drums and a thin sheet of metal, now riddled with bullet holes. On the ground behind was a burnt-out patch of black from the old tires. I looked out past the barricade towards the positions where the Israeli soldiers had stationed themselves, and then wandered over, standing where they must have been only a few hours earlier, staring down the Hebron Road, facing a hail of stones, Molotov cocktails and hatred.

We found out later that an Israeli border guard, Yosef Madhat, had been killed that afternoon in the West Bank town of Nablus. He had been shot in the neck and the Palestinians refused to allow an ambulance to get to him to treat his wounds. The nineteen-year-old boy had slowly bled to death in front of his colleagues.

On our way back to the college, we stopped to talk to people in the street. An elderly man sat on an old chair outside his house. He was desperately unhappy: "The soldiers were shooting at the boys' heads and they were

using live ammunition. They were shooting to kill. What
can we do? There is nothing here for us. We are powerless
against them – and they just bleed us dry of everything we
have." He continued in this way for some time, not angry
with us, but needing an outlet for his powerful emotions.
We listened sympathetically, until his son appeared from
the house, embarrassed by the extent of his father's tirade.
He too was clearly shocked. Usually the Israeli soldiers are
instructed to use rubber bullets and aim for the boys' legs in
order to minimize fatalities. It seemed as if the unwritten
rules had been broken and the Palestinians were angry.

Later that evening, we picked up our luggage and walked
out of the college gate along the Hebron Road, towards
Rachel's Tomb and the checkpoint beyond it, my big bag
slung between us. I remember we were laughing, relieved at
the thought of leaving for a few days' peace in the desert. The
streetlights weren't working and the darkness swallowed us
up. Suddenly the sound of gunfire broke out just over to our
left, cutting through the silence of the night. I swung round
as the dogs began to bark at the disturbance and noticed a
group of young men huddled into a doorway behind us.
They shouted and gestured frantically, beckoning us to come
back along the road. We hurried back to the college gate just
as the sound of automatic rifle fire started off to our left once
more. Someone had rewritten the rules yet again.

Bishara heard us return and came over to the gate where
we were standing, his face a mask of anxiety. "Girls, it's not
safe, it's not safe out there," he repeated. All the same, he
agreed to help us try and leave Bethlehem by another route
and we climbed into his car, praying desperately for safety.
We turned right out of the Bible College, and then swung
left towards the center of town where the streets were
humming with people who were shouting and running
around. Palestinian Authority police were trying to direct
traffic and manage the chaos. As our car turned left into
Manger Street, the policemen began calling after us and
waving us back. One of them ran over to the car and bent
down to the window, saying, "Please don't go that way.

There are Israeli snipers at the end of Manger Street and Hebron Road and we understand they are shooting to kill.'' I felt cold inside – if we had continued along the Hebron Road to the border just now, we would have driven right into the lethal sniper fire.

Our schedule was thrown up in the air. The next day, we did manage to make our way to the Sinai desert, but as I mentioned earlier, we missed the Musalaha group. Perhaps it was just as well, for we managed to get a couple of days' rest instead. We were certainly grateful for it when we returned to the West Bank and discovered that the situation had worsened. Bethlehem was eerily quiet and it felt as if the whole town was under siege. When dusk fell, Selwa told us not to leave any lights shining in the exterior windows and to close the shutters tightly, in case we unwittingly provided a target. Fortunately the new guest wing was built around a central seating area that was totally enclosed, so we could sit in the lounge with the Bible College volunteers and talk. All of the other guests staying at the college had left the West Bank.

The television was tuned in to one of the local Palestinian news stations which was showing hideous close up images of boys and men being shot in the face and head. As their bodies were handled into the ambulances, a cry would go up from the other boys grouped around – *"Allahu Akhbar"* – God is great: another martyr, another hero wounded for the cause. All the while, the channel played Islamic chants, stirring the Palestinians to revenge. It was difficult to tear our eyes away from the scenes repeated over and over again, sometimes in slow motion. We watched for a while longer, and then somebody got up to switch the television off, leaving the rest of us sitting stunned in our seats. I realized that the effect these images had had on us was overpoweringly negative, filling us with fear. Some of the footage had showed Israeli Apache helicopters slamming missiles into the walls of Palestinian Authority buildings in Gaza. Locals in Bethlehem were saying a civilian house in Beit Sahour, a village just south of Bethlehem, had accidentally been hit by one of these missiles the day before, killing a small baby. We later found out the story was true.

The next morning was a Friday and we woke up to discover that the West Bank had been sealed off as the Palestinians called for a "Day of Rage". The mosques were packed for the Friday morning services and around Bethlehem the loudspeakers on top of the minarets broadcast angry sermons from the Imams. Inside the Bible College, we waited for the services to come to an end, fearful of what would happen afterwards. The air felt bitter as I stood outside hanging up washing on the line in the morning sunshine.

When the services ended, people poured out of the mosques onto the streets. We stood inside the college gates, watching as a huge crowd of demonstrators marched past us towards Rachel's Tomb, this time headed up by a line of black-robed Catholic priests and Muslim clerics, linked arm in arm. Behind them a young man in an electric wheelchair motored along, a Palestinian flag held aloft in his hand. Other people in the crowd who were wearing black headscarves over their faces with tiny slits for their eyes, had tied Israeli flags to their ankles, dragging them along the ground and trampling them underfoot as an insult to the Israeli soldiers. When they got to the border, they set fire to the flags, chanting angry slogans. I think the demonstration was meant to be peaceful, but it soon degenerated into the endless cycle of stones and bullets once more. As the ambulance sirens pierced the air and the smell of tear gas permeated everywhere, we retreated inside and waited for the fighting to end. On the news, Ehud Barak, the then Israeli Prime Minister, was offering the Palestinians the first ultimatum of the second *intifada* – stop the fighting by Monday or the tanks will move in.

The next few days were marked either by the presence or absence of fighting. On the peaceful days, we hurried out to do some shopping or visited friends to check on how they were doing. We lived in a daze, unsure of how to restructure our time, shocked by the events we had witnessed. Eventually we decided to spend a few extra days in the West Bank, visiting the Christians we knew to encourage them and see if there were any ways in which we could help.

One afternoon, during a lull in the hostilities, we made a brief trip to Jerusalem in order to change our travel arrangements. We had intended to take the bus to the Egyptian border at Rafah in the Gaza Strip and then drive on to Cairo, but heavy fighting in Gaza meant that was impossible.

Jerusalem had undergone a similar transformation to Bethlehem. In the streets, nobody was smiling. People hurried about their business with drawn, unhappy faces, reluctant to linger outside in case some incident occurred. Salim told us that in some areas of the city, where traditionally Jews and Arabs had lived peacefully side by side, tensions were now surfacing and outbreaks of violence occurring. People were shocked at how quickly the whole situation had degenerated and were utterly confused. Until a few days ago, you could tell the places and times that trouble would occur. Now it was much harder to predict. It was as if somebody had opened the stopper and let out the genie and now nobody could put it back again. The downward spiral had begun with a vengeance.

We called into the travel agency, where the agents were longstanding friends. At the front of the shop, a metal grille was half pulled over the entrance, ready to be slammed shut at the first sign of trouble. Gaby jumped out of his chair as we eased past the grille, a smile creasing his face.

"I am so glad to see you! It's good you are safe. How is Bet Lehem – crazy huh? Now, we must fix something for you. Rafah is impossible I'm afraid. You can take the plane from Tel Aviv to Cairo yes? You are lucky – you can leave all this!" Gaby gestured at the street outside. "Now, tell me, what is the situation in Bet Lehem?" In common with everybody else, Gaby traded news, supplementing the Palestinian and Israeli propaganda on the television with hard information from friends and acquaintances.

While his colleague was sorting out our plane tickets,
Gaby joked, handing us a present of a box of dates each.
"Now you can say to your friends you had a date in
Jerusalem no? They will be jealous of you!" We laughed
along with him, but for all of us, our laughter was tinged
with sadness. We recognized an almost desperate need to
negate the fear and unhappiness but it was an impossible
task.

"How's business?" I asked Gaby, and then immediately
wished I hadn't. His face clouded over. "It's bad," he
replied. "Everybody has cancelled their travel arrangements. The Western governments are issuing negative
travel warnings. Now, there are no tourists."

The bus back to Bethlehem was full of Arab women, their
bags and shopping baskets heavy with fruit and vegetables.
Stocks in the West Bank shops were getting low and people
took advantage of every break in the fighting to get fresh
food.

In the afternoon, we made good on an earlier promise to
visit a Christian lady who lives right on the front line near
one of the flashpoints. As we approached Warda's house,
the smell of gas was overpowering. Quite clearly there was a
major leak somewhere nearby and Warda was anxious. "It's
been on the local news," she told us. "They hit a gas tank,
and now the gas is leaking everywhere. How it didn't
explode when they hit it ... they've told everybody don't
start shooting here today. I hope not or ..." she shrugged
her shoulders.

We sat drinking juice and asked Warda how she was
coping. "I'm so scared, I haven't been out of my house for
over a week," she told us. "My husband and I came here
when we were first married, so I don't want to move. This is
my family house, but it's terrible here. Once we had land
over there on Abu Ghneim," she said, pointing in the
direction of the Israeli Har Homa settlement, which is
situated on a hillside just outside Bethlehem, "but the
Israelis confiscated it from us. I have a friend who is an
Israeli soldier. He phoned me the other day from his mobile

and he told me, 'I'm standing on your land'. He sympath-
ized with me. I just said to him, please don't shoot any
Arabs on my land. That would make me very sad."

Warda shivered, and then she stood up to show us the
bullet holes that riddled the walls of the living room where
we were now sitting. Just as she did so, one of her teenage
sons came into the room and sat down with us. Warda
glanced at him nervously and put her hand protectively on
his arm: "I am scared every time my sons leave the house.
We are a Christian family and we don't want to join in
throwing stones, but the Israeli soldiers don't know that. I
am frightened they will shoot at my boys. It's difficult with
our own people too. When there is fighting, they hide in
our doorway, and they bang on the door asking for a drink
of water. We used to give them a drink, but then once,
when we did so, the Israeli soldiers came running into my
house, chasing them. I was terrified. Now, when the fighting is bad, we all go downstairs into the cellar and wait."

We spoke for a while longer, but it was clear that Warda
was on edge. "Please don't misunderstand me," she said
finally. "I am so glad you have come to visit me. To have
people come here in all this fighting, it is really something.
But it's risky for me that you are here. We are a Christian
family and the Muslims say we are not part of them, but we
are Palestinian. When I have foreigners here, my neighbors
are suspicious. They think we are Zionists and siding with
the Americans."

That night – like most of the nights I spent in the West
Bank that October, I slept only fitfully. From dusk until
dawn, Israeli planes droned overhead, using sophisticated
surveillance equipment to track the movements of the
Palestinian fighters in the streets below. From time to time,
we heard the unmistakable thudding of the rotors of an
Apache attack helicopter. Each time it passed over us I
winced, wondering if a missile would come slamming
through our walls. Occasionally, sporadic bursts of machine
gun fire would break out across the valley, followed by the
inevitable cacophony of dogs barking at the noise.

Before we went to sleep each night, we read from the
Psalms, and the age-old words of David, pursued by his
enemies, brought us some measure of peace:

> *"When I am afraid,*
>   *I will trust in you.*
> *In God, whose word I praise,*
>   *in God I trust; I will not be afraid.*
>   *What can mortal man do to me?"*   (Psalm 56:3–4)

We woke up one Sunday morning to complete stillness.
The gunfire had drifted away with the dawn and the birds
were singing. We decided to attend the small Palestinian
church that meets in the Bible College buildings. I sat at the
back of the meeting hall and let the beautiful Arabic
worship songs soak over me. It felt like a taste of heaven
in the midst of hell. The pastor, Nihad Salman, spoke
gently to the congregation, aware of the suffering and fear
in everybody's hearts. "Please, don't watch the television,"
he told us, referring to the endless footage of fighting and
death. "Where is our source of comfort? For the last two
weeks we've all been through hard times. Does the television comfort you? Two days ago I watched the television
and I went like I was crazy. All the programs are encourag-
ing people to fight. The devil wants us to get angry. I told
God I was sorry and I turned to my Bible. How can we
comfort people around us if we don't get our comfort from
God? We must be a light in this darkness for others around
us so that they can see their way through the darkness. It's
not helpful to see the violence and hatred and it makes us
lose perspective. Please, read your Bibles instead. Let God's
peace soak into your hearts. And pray for forgiveness. Pray
for the Israelis and pray for our people here too. You don't
know what will happen to them. Maybe God will give you
an opportunity to tell them about His peace when they are
so scared."

I was impressed with Nihad's words. They made sense
and brought perspective back into our shattered lives. After

the service, we spent some time talking with him about his work in Bethlehem. He was a man of utter conviction and a strong faith.

"I studied in Germany and in the United States," Nihad told me. "I ministered in different ministries there and saw how God used me and brought fruit from my work. Then I felt the call of God, which was placed on my heart since I was a young boy, to go back to the land, to the West Bank, to minister. From 1991 until 1997 I was pastor of a church here, but there was only one family who came! Can you imagine? I learnt during that time that success before God has nothing to do with numbers, but with our faithfulness to the vision that He has given us. I knew God was calling me to be faithful to the task of preaching here, whatever the results and whatever the cost. Once I was speaking with friends, and they said, 'Be careful there is shooting next to your house, in the street.' I said to them, 'I will not be killed until I finish what God has told me to do.' All the same, it was a struggle to preach to so few people year after year and finally one day I came to God and said, 'I don't know what you are doing here, but I put my trust in you. What you are happy with, I am happy with. If you are happy with one family in this church, then I am happy with one family.' You know, after that people began to come into the church and we saw God's blessing. Now we have about twenty-three families in the church and just this summer I baptized thirty people in the Jordan River. I would say eighty percent of this church is made up of new believers."

We talked about the difficulties of leading a church in such a volatile part of the world. How did Nihad encourage his congregation to forgive and to go on forgiving in the middle of violence, fear and hatred?

"Yesterday, the son of one of our elders heard that his good friend got shot. The boy is now bitter towards the Jews, asking why did they do this? Why did they kill my friend? I said to the elder, 'Johnny, let's pray that God will give you wisdom how to deal with your child. It is very important to take away that hurt and hatred. Talk to him about the love of Jesus; let him know there are things that we don't understand. Let him say, I don't understand but I know one thing, let us pray for the family of that victim, let us pray that this violence will be stopped.'"

Nihad looked up, his gaze penetrating, "You know, this violence here, it's not just something on the street. It is in your house. Your children, when they grow up they see it all around them, so it is very important to deal with it and to be close to God. We need real wisdom – what to say, how to react. I had a man in my church – his father had been killed by the Israeli soldiers. This young man had so much hatred. He became a Christian and he told me that he accepted that the Lord loves him, but he couldn't understand that God was asking him to love his enemies. I said, 'Okay, this needs to change in your heart. Are you open to that? To ask God to take away the bitterness and give you love? You can't do it yourself.' But that young guy, until now he refused that God would even change his heart. He wants that hatred. He feels that if he loves the Jews, he will lose the loyalty he has to his father. He loved his father. He was a young boy when his father got killed in front of his eyes, next to the house; he was in the doorway, and his father was on the street. Standing there one minute, the next, gunned down. It is not easy – we have to rely on God's help, we cannot do it. I cannot place love in the heart of a person, to take away hatred and bitterness, even bitterness towards God. Only God can do that."

On our last morning in the West Bank, I went into the Bible College library to send a few emails. I spoke for a while with the librarian, a friendly Palestinian lady in her early thirties. She told me that she lives with her young family in Beit Jala, where the fighting had been very intense over the past few days. "I have a four-year-old daughter," she said. "My little girl is so scared. Two days ago our neighbor's house was hit by bullets. Last night, my daughter said to me, 'Mummy, please pray we are safe tonight.' I prayed and then she asked me, 'Mummy, please pray some more.' The next morning we woke up and our house was safe. My daughter said to me, 'God heard our prayers. None of the red stones hit our house.' It's funny, she doesn't understand what bullets are. She thinks the red tracer fire from the soldiers' guns are stones."

For me, the saddest thing in the whole situation was the suffering of the children. Earlier that day, I'd visited Fawzi, a shopkeeper who owns a souvenir shop in Manger Street. We would often call in at his shop when we were in Bethlehem and he unfailingly made coffee for us and sat with us to talk. That day, a Palestinian Authority soldier was in the shop too. We were immediately made to feel welcome and we asked how they felt about the situation. The soldier was beside himself. The day before, a young boy called Mohammed al-Durrah had been caught in the cross-fire with his father in the middle of a street in Gaza. The boy was shot and died in his father's arms. "You know," said the soldier, "on the Western news, they criticize us for our fighting. But what can we do when things like that are happening? It happens even with the animals. If you have a cat and attack the kittens, the cat will really go for you. They are hurting our children. We can't stand back and do nothing."

Fawzi too was distressed. "At home, I found my children hiding behind the fridge. They didn't want to come out. I asked them why, and they said they are scared the heli-copters will shoot at our house."

In the street outside, I passed a group of little boys playing in a garden with wooden guns. They had tied their T-shirts around their faces, just like their older brothers. Empty bullet cartridges, collected from the streets, had been tied onto their wooden guns. As I took a photograph of them, they posed for me in delight, toy rifles in the air, arms lifted high in a parody of the real fighters. I remem-bered Salim's words, "By the age of five, children here have a very clear idea of who the 'enemy' is." I wondered if there would ever be any way out for them.

Chapter 6

The Garden Tomb

"The holiness of the people precedes the holiness of the land. There is no mystical significance to land. There is only a significance to what human beings do. Holiness in Judaism does not come from stones or books. It comes from you and me and how we live here and now."

(Rabbi Hartman, quoted in *From Beirut to Jerusalem* by Thomas L. Friedman)

It was time for us to leave the West Bank and head on into Jerusalem. I left Bethlehem with mixed emotions, desperate to get away from the daily shootings, the tension that permeated everywhere and the drone of helicopters and planes hovering above our heads every night. I was exhausted and deeply shocked by the events of the past few weeks. I had friends on both sides of this conflict and the sudden degeneration into hostilities was deeply personal. It would be months, even years, before I could watch a news bulletin on Israel and the West Bank without that sense of shock and anguish returning.

At the same time, I felt a deep sadness and guilt at leaving my Palestinian friends behind. Many of them didn't have the necessary permits to leave the West Bank, let alone the country. They were forced to stick it out, seeing their quality of life become daily more precarious and depressing. I have an enormous amount of respect for people like Bishara and

Selwa, who could easily emigrate to the States – they already have the necessary documents – but instead they have chosen to live and serve their people in the West Bank. As they waved us off, I remembered that Bishara once told us how demoralizing it was for the Palestinian Christians during the Gulf War when the majority of Western missionaries began to pull out during the increase in hostilities. As our taxi pulled away from the Bible College, I felt guilty and could barely meet their eyes to say goodbye.

Sometimes I dream about the Bethlehem I once visited – where the streets were peaceful and you could wander around, laughing and joking with the shopkeepers and people on the street corners. The Bethlehem, where a family once invited us to share their lunch, even though we had only stopped to ask for directions. Where teenage boys partied on Christmas Eve and schoolchildren chatted to you about their hopes and dreams.

But perhaps that Bethlehem was an illusion too. Even in the late 1990s, an ever-increasing despair was rising up under the semblance of comparative peace. The poor economy and lack of facilities were forcing many Palestinians abroad. Israeli settlements were taking more and more precious land from the West Bank inhabitants. Bethlehem hasn't slumbered for years. Its people have suffered for a long time, sometimes quietly and at other times more forcefully.

In part, my reasons for desiring peace in Israel and the West Bank were selfish. I wanted to be able to come and go as I pleased, to wander around Bethlehem, soaking up its rich atmosphere. But the cry of the Palestinians is far more profound; to be able to farm their own land, make an honest living and to live in peace once more. I have never met anybody – Palestinian or Jew – who really believed that could come to pass.

And so we left, passing the gardens of Tantur as we drew away from the checkpoint, heading straight on for Jerusalem. Driving through the suburbs of the city, I began to feel lonely and isolated. I missed the small-town community where we had shared so much over the past few weeks.

And more curiously, I felt afraid. Far more so than when I was in the West Bank. There, it was relatively easy during the day to predict where the trouble would occur. The flashpoints, such as Rachel's Tomb or the valley by Beit Jala, were identifiable, and providing you kept away after dusk or when there were demonstrations, you were relatively safe. Although you were never entirely immune from a stray sniper bullet or helicopter missile.

In Jerusalem, and in particular, Jewish West Jerusalem, nobody had any idea where the danger would come from. Suicide bombers strike randomly – in crowded cafés, on buses and in busy markets. Every Arab face in the crowd is a potential enemy.

Because of this, we had arranged to stay in a hotel in Palestinian East Jerusalem. Our friends at the travel agency had made the booking for us, saying, "The hotel is run by a Christian family. They will look after you and let you know where there is trouble. You will be safe there."

We drove into East Jerusalem, our taxi driver scouting around for the hotel which we finally discovered tucked away in a narrow side street. The taxi drew up in front of an old colonial-style building with a large courtyard garden. Next to the hotel, a grapevine had been trained over a small terrace, providing welcome shelter from the heat. At the back of the garden, small fountains sparkled in the sun-light, amidst a wealth of green foliage and exotic blooms. After we had checked in our luggage, we sat under the canopy and drank lemon juice, luxuriating in the peace and quiet.

Now we had room to think, it seemed as if we were further away than ever from our aim of getting to know more Jewish people. I was frustrated by the fact that I had spent far more time in the West Bank than I had done in Israel. I was all too aware that I hadn't had as many opportunities to speak and stay with Jews, as I had with Palestinians, in order to get a better understanding of their viewpoint. Each time I visited the Holy Land, I tried to keep a balance. It is far too easy to sympathize with one side or another, but in reality there is injustice and pain on both sides. I think the danger is particularly strong for Christians. Some of us reverence the Jews as God's "chosen people" almost to the point of becoming oblivious to the injustices committed against the Palestinians, among whom there are a number of godly Christians. Others amongst us take up the cry of the Palestinian cause, but in doing so, perhaps forget that many Jews in Israel also want a peaceful solution for their Palestinian neighbors, and themselves hate the unjust methods used at times by the Israeli government. Maybe too, they forget the full horror of some of the atrocities committed by the militant Palestinians. If we are expecting and praying for Christians on both sides to exercise forgiveness and understanding, how can we do any less?

I lay on my bed in the hotel, trying to get some rest, but every time I closed my eyes my mind felt like the Palestinian television station, endlessly replaying all the scenes I'd witnessed during the course of the past few weeks. I gave up and we decided to take a walk into West Jerusalem, along the Ben Yehuda Street. While Sian joined a long and slow-moving queue for a cash-point machine, I walked over to a balcony and looked down on the busy thoroughfare just below us. It was a Wednesday night and it seemed as if everybody in the city was out on the town, determined to enjoy themselves. I wondered whether this was in part a reaction to the deteriorating situation. It was almost as if the Jews themselves, feeling vulnerable and anxious, were determined to live life to the full. Although the Jewish occupation of the West Bank is a far more visible thing, at times trapping the entire Palestinian community within its borders when they are sealed, perhaps the Jews too are trapped in a different way. All the soldiers, weaponry and equipment that Israel has at its disposal are unable to keep out the suicide bombers. The Jewish community may have far more than its Palestinian neighbors in terms of economic prosperity, freedom of movement and opportunities for personal progress but they can never enjoy them in peace.

As if to prove the point, two young girls in military uniform came and stood on the balcony next to me, waving at friends in the street below. I felt increasingly uneasy, aware that in the past, militant Palestinians have particularly targeted soldiers. I found myself scanning the crowd for a suspicious face, wondering if we would get unlucky that night and feel the brunt of a suicide bomber's revenge. Somebody tapped my shoulder and I jumped with shock – it was Sian, who had finished with the cash-point machine.

"Let's go and get something to eat," she suggested and I agreed. It was early evening, but the busy shopping streets were thronged with people browsing through the boutiques that remained open. Café tables, set out on the wide pavements, were filled with young people talking and eating. We found a free table and ordered ice creams, but when they arrived I was shocked. The portions were huge and could have fed a whole group of us. Having just come from the West Bank, where people were struggling to obtain even the most basic foods, it was almost too much to take in, and I could barely swallow the ice cream. I didn't blame the Israelis, but I could understand how difficult it must be for Palestinians working in Israel to be faced constantly with the kind of luxuries that they could never afford for their families. We walked back to the hotel, past a market surrounded with police. They were checking identity cards at the entrance, not taking any risks. I was glad to get back to our room, and breathed a sigh of relief. I couldn't imagine how it must feel to spend your life, day in day out, never knowing where the next bomb will go off. During the night, I was woken up several times by an outburst of sirens, and once by gunfire. Each time, I lay in the blackness, wondering what was happening. Even if I had switched on the television set, I couldn't have understood the Hebrew. I was reliant on the World Service bulletins and word of mouth, and I learnt the irony that often, people outside the country are far better informed than those inside.

In a last ditch attempt to retrieve the shreds of our original itinerary, we had telephoned Salim a couple of days earlier and asked if he could help us locate a Messianic Jew who had attended a Musalaha desert trip and who would be happy to talk to us. The next day, we found ourselves speaking with "Miriam", an Israeli in her early twenties who lived and worked in Jerusalem. I was eager to know how she managed to live in the middle of this kind of tension:

"It's scary, very scary," was her forthright reply. "Because you know it hits so randomly and now civilians too. It could easily be your mom on her way to work or your brother with the army – you never know who is hurt. It could be any number of your friends. The first thing you do after an attack is you call everybody you know and make sure that no one was there. You feel almost violated, because it's something that seems so random. That's a terrible feeling. Like the explosions on Ben Yehudah Street. My friend was there and saw it from the window of the place where she worked. She had just walked into the building when the explosion happened, and it has really affected her. I have another friend who lived in Tel Aviv at the time when one of the bombs went off at the Dizengoff Center there. He saw the explosion – and bits of bodies flying everywhere. It's something that never leaves you. It leaves fears with you that you aren't even aware of sometimes. At the moment my brother is in the army. As of now, he hasn't been involved in any of the riots, which I'm very happy about. He's up on the Lebanese border – two of his colleagues were just kidnapped by Hezbollah. That was rather disturbing. We pray for him a lot."

We had arranged to meet Miriam at a Messianic congregation building in West Jerusalem. When we arrived I realized with surprise I'd been to the building before, on my first trip to Israel. Cindy had invited us along to celebrate Hannukah with the congregation. It had been a memorable evening. Party games and fun had been balanced around a beautiful worship service and I'd been deeply moved to hear the Messianic Christians singing plaintive melodies in Hebrew about Jesus their Messiah.

Miriam was waiting for us outside the building, looking somewhat ill at ease. I didn't blame her, she had no real idea of who we were or what we represented and in a country where everybody has a different agenda, you quickly learn to size people up before you choose to share with them.

I was glad to discover that Miriam had grown up in Israel – there are so many immigrants in this country it was interesting to get a chance to talk to somebody who had been born and raised there. Miriam's parents met on a coastal kibbutz just north of Tel Aviv. Her mother became a believer in Jesus there through the witness of her father, and a year or so later they married and moved to Jerusalem. Miriam described her life growing up in a Messianic Jewish family in Jerusalem:

"My parents were generally right wing – most Messianic Jews that live in Israel are supportive of the right wing. So that's what I grew up in and that was my opinion, because that was my parents' opinion. I didn't know very many Arab people. At that time, the congregation I went to was probably more affiliated with the Jewish side rather than the Arab side. So that was the kind of people I was with. I think that has a lot to do with your opinions, because when you grow up thinking the other side is wrong and you are justified and you don't know many people from the other side – you don't even know their stories except for what you hear on the news, which isn't exactly objective – then you don't feel much compassion for them."

But Miriam's experiences have led her to a different position: "As time has gone on, my opinions have changed in meeting people and in hearing their stories," she told us. "Possibly because I am in an environment that encourages more understanding of the Palestinian side. Now I have disagreements with my parents from time to time. I guess they are less trusting of the whole story of the peace process. I'm not completely trusting of it either. I don't know what people's intentions are, especially in politics. You know politicians sometimes use things for their own gain, so the peace process itself, maybe I don't trust as much, but I think it's important for there to be an understanding between the people as much as there can be. So we argue and disagree and present points and we vote differently. They get frustrated with me because they think I'm a little bit too idealistic and I'm kind of forgetting the past and what has taken place before and they think I'm not taking everything into account."

Miriam's comments struck a chord. I had just been reading New York Times correspondent Thomas Friedman's excellent book, *From Beirut to Jerusalem*, in which he discusses the failure of the Palestinians and Israelis to make any significant headway towards a peaceful solution to the conflict. One reason, he argues, is the inability of the Jews to move on from the events of the Holocaust:

> "The tragedy and the irony of the Zionist revolution is that ... it failed to eradicate the collective self-image of the Jews as victim. Although they can now speak their own language and walk with their heads held high, many Israelis today still feel as though they are victims of circumstance and living on borrowed time as much as any Jewish ghetto dwellers in history. They have not really broken out of the prison of their past. That is why, despite the fact that Israel has one of the most powerful and advanced armies and airforces in the world, the country's leadership finds it almost impossible to imagine bold ways in which they could unilaterally use their overwhelming power to shape new options for themselves, particularly regarding the West Bank and Gaza. They still see themselves as a people who react to history rather than shape it."

If Miriam is typical of her generation, then maybe there is a glimmer of hope for the future. She wasn't saying that the Holocaust had to be buried, but that her generation wants to move away from the restraints that bind the older Jews. However, if the young people, both Palestinian and Israeli, are to ever move on, they will have to make a quantum leap away from the propaganda they are fed by their societies. Israel will not let its children forget the Holocaust. The atrocities securely locked in the national consciousness, are reinforced in countless ways. For example, when each Jew carries out their compulsory military service, they are taken to the Holocaust museum in Jerusalem. The message: *Now you have the ability to fight. We will not let this thing happen again at all costs*, echoes through their training.

Thomas Friedman refuses to let the Palestinians off the hook either. Earlier in his book, he comments:

> "Maybe the most important reason Israeli leaders tended to avoid answering the question about what to do with the West Bank and Gaza was that ... the Arabs never gave the Israelis the feeling that they could leave these territories and still maintain their security, hence most Israelis were ready to stay at any price."

Today, there is documented evidence of Palestinian training camps for young freedom fighters. Some Arab children are encouraged to think of the glory associated with a suicide attack. The Palestinian media encourages revenge and anti-Jewish feeling. Peer pressure on youngsters to join in the stone throwing is intense. It is seen as an honorable thing to fight for their country.

For Miriam, as for many others, the journey towards understanding and reconciliation came when she could begin to put real faces to people from the other side. Her first encounter with Palestinians was in her early teens at camps run by the Baptist Church. Miriam attended an Arabic-speaking camp, helping as a volunteer in the kitchen. "All you need to know is just one person, and all of a sudden the whole thing changes," was her observation.

Miriam befriended some of the Arab Christians she met at the camp and kept in touch with them for a while. Two of her friends even went to Jordan to study Arabic, so that they could relate to the Palestinians in a less threatening way – many Palestinians are on edge when they hear Hebrew spoken – to them it is the language of their oppressors. Miriam's friends encouraged her to participate in a Musalaha desert trip, but it proved complicated: "Because I had only just finished my military service, I wasn't allowed to go to Jordan or Egypt where they were doing the trip. If you are on active service in the army, you aren't allowed to leave the country at all. But if you have served in intelligence, which I did, you can't go to Arab countries for a certain period of time afterwards either," she explained to me.

When she finally made it to the desert, a surprise was waiting for Miriam. One of the Arab girls in her group turned out to be the younger sister of a girl she had met some years previously at the Baptist camps. Now Miriam's sister has become a good friend of the girl and she and Miriam go together to visit the girl and her family in Nazareth. Nazareth is in Israel and the Arabs who live there have Israeli citizenship, but all the same, Miriam and her sister are stepping across a cultural and emotional divide to visit their Arab friends. I asked her if it was dangerous for them to do so:

"In Nazareth? No, it's not," she replied. "The only maybe threatening part of it is the culture being different and not knowing if you are offending someone by doing something a certain way. Sometimes there's misunderstanding because they don't understand certain cultural issues in the way you do. There is some awkwardness, of course, when the political situation is bad as it is now. I've been in contact with a girl from Nazareth whose uncle was hurt in the fighting. Another girl who was with us on our trip had a relative that was also hurt in the fighting and just talking about that is difficult. She's gotten very involved in taking lots of pictures and putting them on a website – and well, my brother's in the army and just the way she talks about the soldiers and I know the way my brother is. It's not like he wants to go out there and hurt people, he has no choice, he has to be in the army. And so, just kind of making generalizations about soldiers and me making generaliza-tions about people who are involved in the riots – that's sometimes an awkward thing. It's kind of a stretching issue – it's not something that means you can't communicate, because we've been communicating about this over the past couple of weeks and just trying to understand what's going on and the suffering that's happening on both sides – I think it's a good sort of stretch."

I wondered what the future held for Miriam and the many thousands of Israelis and Palestinians who genuinely want to see a peaceful and just solution to the conflict that has ripped their societies apart for so many years. But do they have enough of a voice in a world that fragments just a little bit more with every stone that is thrown and every bullet that's fired? Each helicopter attack or suicide bomb leaves behind it a fresh layer of fear and mistrust. Fear that isn't dissipated in the breeze like tear gas, but is instead nurtured by the propaganda of the respective governments. It hangs around in the national consciousness like the burnt-out Israeli jeeps that still lie here and there on the roadside; relics from fighting that took place years ago. As far as the political leaders on both sides are concerned, their countries are at war – the conflict has become their whole raison d'etre and has subsumed any other more worthy aim of the nation states.

When you look on a map, you can see how the West Bank is slowly being swallowed up by Israel, squeezed into increasingly smaller enclaves by Israeli bulldozers to make way for a new settlement, highway or "security zone". Many of these settlements are not built randomly – the locations are carefully selected to limit the expansion of Palestinian villages nearby. Sometimes I wonder if I am seeing the slow, agonizing death of the Palestinian nation. If so, the Zionists will have what they want – the lands of "Judea and Samaria" – but at what price?

Few if any of the Palestinians and Israelis I encountered on my travels had any real hope that Arafat and Sharon are the men who will bring peace to this part of the world. The impression I received from the people I met on both sides, Christians, Jews, Muslims and secularists, was of two nations jaded by political rhetoric and endless finger pointing. It is no accident that Islamic fundamentalism and ultra-orthodox Judaism are on the increase – desperate people are seeking desperate measures to find some way forward out of the gridlock in which they find themselves.

I left Miriam with mixed feelings, excited by her positive attitude towards the Palestinians, but questioning whether the contribution of people like her would ever be enough to turn the situation around. There was only one more place I wanted to visit, and there I hoped to find some way of processing everything I had learned on my trips to Israel. There was nowhere else left to go.

The Garden Tomb is totally unlike many of the holy places in Israel and the West Bank. Instead of the usual jealously guarded church or shrine, this particular site is surrounded by a beautiful garden under the administration of the Garden Tomb Association. There is a strong argument for this being the actual location where the body of Jesus was brought after His crucifixion, but even if this is not so, the cave tomb gives a vivid idea of the place where Jesus was buried.

The garden has been designed for contemplation and we followed a pathway that led us through gentle vistas and shady walks. After a while, the pathway crossed over a bridge spanning an old watercourse and there in front of us was the tomb; a simple semicircular structure which had been hewn out of the cream-colored rock face. In front of its little wooden doorway was a long channel where the round gravestone would once have been rolled to seal the tomb after burial.

I stepped into the cool recesses of the tomb. To the right hand side of the small chamber was a raised platform of rock where the body would have been placed, wrapped in its grave cloths and anointed with precious oils and incense. I thanked God that the story which had begun only a few miles away in Bethlehem, hadn't ended here in this cold tomb. The fact that Jesus, the Son of the Living God, rose from the dead and is alive today turns this book – and the lives of the people I have interviewed – around.

In every gesture of love demonstrated by the Palestinian Christians and Messianic Jews in this land, in every move towards the other side, every effort towards forgiveness, God is the life force: healing broken hearts, bringing grace and courage to live beyond the ordinary. It may well be that we will not see a political solution to the Middle East crisis in our lifetimes – or ever. But God hasn't stopped showing us His solution – the path of love and forgiveness. His response is to transform and heal lives in the middle of pain and suffering, just as His Son Jesus did, over two thousand years ago.

I recently received an email from a Christian who has been working in the Holy Land during some of the worst fighting. He wrote:

> "I believe we must all focus on the one thing for which we have been called – the Kingdom of God. What this world needs, now as always, is Christians who are committed to working for the advancement of the Kingdom of God. There are no military or political or economic solutions for sin and the state of the human soul, which is what lies at the root of all the world's ills and woes. The task of spreading the Kingdom of God and His dominion throughout the world has been given to us, the Body of Christ – there is no 'Plan B'. Therefore let us be certain that we are walking in the footsteps of our Lord and Savior."

As I sat in front of the Garden Tomb and thought of all the people I had met in Israel and the West Bank, I felt humbled. I knew that I had never yet been called to make the kind of sacrifices and decisions that many of them make daily – I don't even know if I could do so. But I do know that I can commit myself to praying for them and to taking a stand against the injustices that I see. And also, I can commit myself to making no judgments, but to understanding and learning, as much as I can, the complexities and challenges of the situations which they face and to give my support, both financial and practical wherever possible. Each time I have left the Holy Land, I have done so a richer person – moved by the grace and sacrificial love I have witnessed from Christians – and others – on both sides of the divide.

If you would like to find out more about the work of Musalaha, you can contact them at the following addresses, or visit their website:

In the UK:
Restorer Trust
St Peter's Parish Centre, 347 Church Road, Bolton,
Lancs BL1 5RR, UK

In the United States:
Reconciliation Ministries
PO Box 238, Medina, WA 98039-0238, USA

In Israel:
Musalaha
PO Box 52110, Jerusalem 91521, Israel

Email: musalaha@netvision.net.il
Website: www.musalaha.org

If you would like more information on the work of Open Doors with Brother Andrew, they can be contacted at:

ODI Development UK
PO Box 129, Witney OX29 6WN, England

Email: odidev@od.org

If you would like more information on the work of Bethlehem Bible College, they can be contacted at:

Bethlehem Bible College
PO Box 17166, Jerusalem 91190, Israel

Email: bethbc@planet.edu

If you have enjoyed this book and would like to help us to send a copy of it and many other titles to needy pastors in the **Third World**, please write for further information or send your gift to:

Sovereign World Trust
PO Box 777, Tonbridge
Kent TN11 0ZS
United Kingdom

or to the **'Sovereign World'** distributor in your country.

Visit our website at **www.sovereign-world.org**
for a full range of Sovereign World books.